ron arad

ron arad

Deyan Sudjic

Laurence King

Published in 1999 by Laurence King Publishing
an imprint of Calmann & King Ltd
71 Great Russell Street
London WC1B 3BN
Tel: +44 171 831 6351
Fax: +44 171 831 8356
e-mail: enquiries@calmann-king.co.uk
www.laurence-king.com

A catalogue record for this book is available
from the British Library.

ISBN 1 85669 126 8

Designed by Silvia Gaspardo Moro and Angus Hyland
Chapter icons and additional design by Imke Himstedt

Commissioned photography by Wilhelm Moser

Printed in Singapore

Photographic Credits

The publisher and author would like to thank the
following photographers and copyright holders for the
use of their material (page numbers are given in
parentheses):

Grisha Arad (46, 50, 63); Simon Bevan (59); Alison
Brooks (90 top left and right, bottom left and right);
Erica Calvi (105); Rene Chavanne (169); Gadi Dagon (79
right, 88, 89 left, 92–3, 97); Richard Davies (18–19, 20,
216–17, 219); Christoph Kicherer (33–35, 60, 79 left,
84, 89 right, 94, 96, 104, 122); Howard Kingsnorth (13,
14, 20, 21, 25–7, 31–2, 63); Tom Miller (173–5, 177);
Wilhelm Moser (24, 44, 47, 54–5, 57–8, 61, 64–7, 72,
83, 148–9, 154–67, 202–11); Alan Mower (90 centre);
Ozzy O'Mara (11); Guido Pedron (150); Alberto Piovano
(100–1); Philippe Ruault (116–18); Oliver Salway (98);
Tom Vack (74–5).

CONTENTS

Introduction   7

01 What I really like about it is that it reminds me a bit of a car seat   8
02 I think I'll keep my Bang & Olufsen   16
03 Shadow of Time   22
04 A new descending staircase   28
05 A Well Tempered chair   36
06 A conversation with Rolf Fehlbaum   42
07 Sticks and stones and Louis Vuitton   48
08 Things people don't really need (but can't afford)   52
09 From Udine to Bologna and back again   68
10 Stefano's bar   76
11 Fitzcarraldo   86
12 The helicopter disappeared into the sky towing the pipe out of the factory   102
    whilst the machine was still extruding it
13 For young people setting up homes, low production costs in the Far East,   108
    selling high design to the market-place etc., etc.
14 We can but wait (optimistically) and see   114
15 Freeze-dried mice next to Puffing Billy   126
16 Sport   132
17 Fantastic Plastic Elastic   140
18 The Ready-to-Wear RTW   146
19 Maybe a hyper-realistic sculpture of one hundred stacking chairs   152
20 It doesn't even have a proper roof   170
21 Call it red tape   180
22 Three-minute eggs   184
23 When will Kartell do it in plastic and what will you do next year?   190
24 B.O.O.P.S   200
25 The Piper project   214

Index   220
Biography   222
Chronology of major works   223

INTRODUCTION

Ron Arad, who began his career as an outsider, occupying the self-invented margins of design with an approach that grew out of improvisation and makeshift methods, has moved to centre stage. He once made objects in his own workshop in tiny batches; now he designs for industrial-scale production. Aesthetically, he was once an idiosyncratic and isolated presence on the edge of the design landscape. His work represented a kind of opposition to the received wisdom of conventional aesthetic responses: it wasn't about taste or high design, and it wasn't about craft values. Now his work is shaping the mainstream. This transformation has taken 20 years, a period which has coincided with a radical shift in perceptions of design, and its place in the wider cultural and economic context. It is a shift in which Arad himself has played an important part. If design since 1980 is a conversation carried on by a succession of participants – from Ettore Sottsass and his Memphis collaborators, to Philippe Starck, and from Alessandro Mendini to Javier Mariscal, and supported by a few vital manufacturers, from Rolf Fehlbaum at Vitra to Alberto Alessi – Ron Arad is one of the very few British-based participants in that conversation. True, there are now more British voices taking part than there were. But Arad was there 20 years ago, and is still there today. He has carved out a special territory for himself which has formed one of the points of reference throughout the period.

Despite its minimal manufacturing base, Britain, or perhaps more accurately, London, has become a significant creative centre for design. Arad is now seen as an important player in British design (he is described as British mainly on the strength of having lived, studied and worked in London since the early 1970s), although until very recently he had a much higher profile in Europe. Collectors of Arad's one-offs are concentrated in Germany. It was the Pompidou Centre in Paris, rather than the Victoria and Albert Museum in London, that mounted a major exhibition of his work. To characterize his work as 'British' design is misleading; it is true that Arad's work exhibits a sense of iconoclasm, invention, wit and independence of mind that might be regarded as specifically British. But it is essentially international in its outlook and audience.

Over the years, the emphasis in Arad's work has changed. He has moved from the pragmatism of a small-scale design studio producing tailor-made functional furniture limited by cost and a lack of the capital needed for elaborate production methods, towards the much greater cultural ambition of producing pieces of furniture that were invested with at least some of the qualities of art. Arad began as an art student, but then studied architecture in London, and his career has explored the difficult territory between art, architecture and design. It has shown a resistance to categorization that has not always been easy. The language of criticism depends on creating a series of self-contained territories. Arad understands each of these territories, but refuses to limit his range of references to one rather than another. Most recently it has been architecture that has preoccupied him, as he has shifted in scale from domestic furniture to larger and more ambitious architectural projects.

It is a shift that has at each stage depended on an appropriate infrastructure. Arad has never been keen to work for other people, but he quickly developed a certain gift for establishing the means of working with people in different ways. Each stage in his career has been marked by a fluctuating cast of collaborators and assistants, and has constantly reconfigured itself to meet the needs of the moment. The only constant figure alongside Arad has been his partner, Caroline Thorman. The surroundings in which the cast has been accommodated have also been precisely tailored to the different needs of each stage of Arad's career. Early on there was a shop, with a tiny design office tacked on at the back. Then there was a shop/showroom with a studio. Then came the showroom-cum-exhibition space with studio. After that a workshop was added to the basic mix, and finally the workshop was dropped to make way for more studio space.

The last 20 years have seen design move from a marginal activity to one that now has a high public profile. The shift has not been an entirely comfortable one for designers because it has seen them sucked into the fashion system, taken up one moment and discarded as old hat shortly afterwards. A series of style fads has come and gone, leaving each looking quaint and dated. Arad has survived the process unscathed. His work has shifted gear. Early on, the way he worked with ready-made objects could be seen as having something to do with high tech. His work then became much more emotionally charged and sculptural. Now Arad is ready to work with the aesthetic values of volume production. Each phase has been based on what he has learned, and represents a progression rather than a rejection. Arad has never repeated himself, and has always moved forward. Now at the peak of his career, he shows no signs of slackening his pace.

07

WHAT I REALLY LIKE ABOUT IT IS THAT IT REMINDS ME A BIT OF A CAR SEAT

A couple of London's smarter auction houses – the kind of places that have made a gentlemanly business over the centuries out of Old Masters and Georgian silver, and which would previously never have contemplated transgressing the line between the antique and the merely second-hand – have discovered a new commodity: design. Ettore Sottsass's Valentine typewriter, once an icon of modernity that sold in its hundreds of thousands and was then banished to the attic and dusty oblivion by the all-conquering personal computer, is now re-emerging to become as much part of the currency of the connoisseur collector's world as an Otto Wagner chair from his Postal Savings Bank. The shift was signalled in the most provocative way when the Rover chair began to feature in the sale room catalogues, complete with comprehensive notes about provenance.

Arad's studio, One Off, was moving out of the glossy world of the Milan Furniture Fair and into the auction houses with remarkable speed. The first time that this happened, even the elapse of a decade between the emergence of a design and its apotheosis in the sale room seemed uncomfortably rapid. Today, the speeded-up process can take less than six months.

The Rover chair was an object that came with a great deal of cultural baggage even before it acquired the curious status of a living antique. It had already had a complex past life, even when it was still 'new'. This was a chair that was the outcome of some inspired creative scavenging. It was the product of a shot-gun wedding between the ready-made leather-upholstered front seats of the Rover 90 – the dumpy Boadicea's chariot of British motoring, a worthy but dull design that was the car of choice for the genteel and elderly at the end of the 1950s – and a proprietary scaffolding system designed for use on muddy building sites. This unlikely pairing was the result of what, initially at least, were ideologically innocent attempts to offer the young and impecunious a chair that had the comfort and the production values of an industrially manufactured piece of furniture, but at a price within reach of bedsit-land. The earliest example of the Rover chair – and the one which commands the highest price in the auction room – came

in red leather. A detail that was a fluke as far as the designer was concerned. 'I didn't know that they weren't all red. I didn't know that red was actually the rarest colour. I just found one in the scrap-yard, it was a bit of luck.'

It was the idea of a car seat, rather than specifically a Rover seat, that was the attraction:

'When I was a student, I had a chair in my living room that was based on a not so nice car seat I had made a frame for. It was never entirely satisfactory, but I can remember saying that there must be lots of ergonomically designed chairs being scrapped all the time, and why not put them to new use. But then when I actually set out to find them, it wasn't quite as easy as that. The first place I went to look was a car dump off the Finchley Road, and as it turned out, there was nothing that was any good. Then I went to another place run by a Greek guy in a scrap-yard behind the Round House [in London's Chalk Farm] and it was there that I bought the seats for the first two Rovers.'

A designer living in Milan at the same stage in his career as Arad's at that point would, more likely than not, have been designing for a furniture manufacturer working on an industrial scale. But it wasn't Milan, it was London that Arad chose as the city in which to study after art school in Israel, a decision that brought with it both advantages, in terms of its creative openness, and drawbacks. Despite all its creative energy, Britain is not a country that is abundantly endowed with furniture manufacturers interested in making anything but the most banal of domestic objects. It is one of the great unexplained mysteries of contemporary culture that for all the scarcity of employers interested in making use of their skills, Britain continues to turn out such large numbers of design graduates. In the early 1980s a large number of them opted for the ultimately self-defeating short-term survival strategy of making objects themselves. The problem is that design and craft are not the same. The visual vocabulary of design in the 1980s was shaped by the possibilities of machine production, not by the imperfections and idiosyncrasies of hand work.

The marketplace was not an option. But Arad's work had nothing to do with the world of craft either. Instead, it was based on a territory all of its own, carved out of the margins of an industrial aesthetic. And while this strategy might not necessarily produce objects that were affordable for a large audience, it would allow for the sophisticated finish and quality of a machine-made product, even if it was so only at one remove.

Despite the readiness of some observers to interpret the One Off workshop as an expression of the craft spirit, craft was never a strategy that was of interest. Recycling ready-mades and using found industrial materials was a more congenial alternative. And with it came some of the resonances of art, a dimension that had always interested Arad. His driving ambition was to find ways to make possible the production of afford-

able artefacts with the sophistication of the industrial world. With it came the possibility of objects that carried meanings on rich and varied levels. The Rover wasn't the first step in the process. It depended for its frame on Kee Klamp, originally patented by a man named Gascoigne in the 1930s as a low-cost steelwork scaffolding system which Arad had already put to ingenious use. In the early days of the first One Off shop in Sicilian Avenue, and then in Covent Garden, Kee Klamp was the mainstay for an entire product range. It readily lent itself to the production of beds, sleeping platforms, tables and storage units as a structural framework that could be configured in an infinite variety of ways. They were functionally ingenious, but it was the Rover chair that brought a brilliantly successful formal resolution to what had previously been essentially technical questions.

The Rover chair was never exactly cheap – even before it got into the sale-room catalogues. Indeed, the first serious customer was not a strapped for cash bedsit dweller, but Jean-Paul Gaultier:

'I came to the shop on Boxing Day 1981, and there was a guy knocking on the door. "Sorry we are closed," I said. "But I want to buy this chair," he said, pointing through the glass. Actually he wanted six. At the time, I had no idea who he was, but he seemed to have a nose for what was in the air.'

The Rover echoes, of course, Marcel Duchamp's ready-mades, as well as the work of the Castiglioni brothers in the shape of the tractor-seat chair, and the Toio floor lamp, based on a band saw, a car head-light and a fishing rod. Less

The Rover chair, 1981. A reclining leather seat reclaimed from a Rover 2-litre car was mounted on a tubular steel and cast iron frame. The first two seats Arad found happened to be red. It was only much later that he realized that red Rover seats were very rare. They therefore now fetch a much higher price at auction.

The Aerial Light (1981).
In this early cable-
connected version the
aerial moved at great
speed due to the lack of
a clutch motor. Later
versions used ultrasonic
remote control and finally
the more efficient infra-
red.

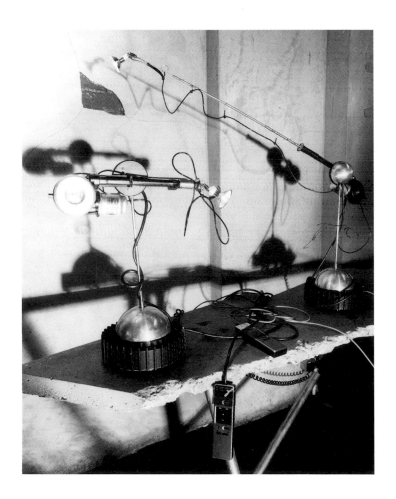

well known as a precedent was an armchair designed by Jean Prouvé in the 1920s, which appears – with its adjustable back, and its leather seat slung in a metal frame – to be a clear precursor of the Rover chair, though it was manufactured from scratch rather than assembled from pre-existing components. In fact, Jean Prouvé himself, with a career that took in a metalworking apprenticeship, as well as periods as a manufacturer, a designer and an architect, is a figure to whom Arad might be seen as owing a certain debt in terms of the possibilities of his career.

The Rover chair opened the way to a series of exuberant experiments with other ready-made found objects. The simplest was a shelving system rigged up using brick-layers' hods purchased from a building equipment supply store. Then there was a stool assembled with a pre-manufactured scooter seat from Puch, the Austrian motorcycle company.

In the same family of objects was the Aerial Light – a ready-made remote-controlled car aerial, transformed into a desk lamp by the addition of a transformer, a diochroic lamp and external power cables. The ready-made featured fingerprints on

the remote control unit, and a patent claim on the base, transferred directly – and intact – from the foot of a sheet of Letraset.

The Transformer, a seating range that relied on a proprietary system for rescuing injured accident victims and developed by Eric Victor, an early mentor of Arad's, went further. It involved a vacuum-formed sealed bag of foam granules that could be shaped to the exact form of the injured body, providing firm support for the spine and allowing the injured person to be safely moved. Collaborating with Victor, Arad put the system to work as a chair and a sofa.

The Aerial Light, 1981. Keypad for the infra-red remote control (above left). The graphics are an extension of the ready-made, ad-hoc approach. The keys are marked by Arad's fingerprints. The handwriting is a Letraset transfer and even the 'patent pending' statement is lifted direct from the small text that appears at the bottom of the Letraset sheet. The Aerial Light is a low-voltage light and contains over 350 parts, many of them ready-mades (opposite). Its omnidirectional extending and retracting arm was adapted from a standard electric car aerial. A clutch motor controls the speed of movement, the arm taking 60 seconds to move through 360 degrees. The halogen bulb conveniently flips over as the arm rotates, ensuring that the light always functions as a down-lighter.

helves × sizes

The Transformer, 1981. The Transformer is an airtight PVC envelope filled with unexpanded polystyrene granules. Air is sucked out with a household vacuum cleaner via a non-return valve, 'freezing' the cushion with the sitter's imprint.

I THINK I'LL KEEP MY BANG & OLUFSEN

When the world's first – and quite possibly last – reinforced concrete record player, complete with equally concrete loudspeakers and amplifier made its appearance, we were all still rather in awe of audio equipment. The price of even the most straightforward stereo system ensured that this was a category of object to be treated with a certain respect. Stereo was precious, and it was expected not just to cost a lot, but to look as if it did too.

And then there was the fetish that hi-fi devotees made of precision. The job of the designer was to signal and celebrate these qualities and not to subvert the genre. The visual language of reliability, quality and seriousness was brushed aluminium and matt-black and necessarily involved elaborate arrays of switches and dials. The major question facing the designer was the precise degree of the radius on the edges of the pre-amplifier, or the tactile quality of the on-off switch, or the infinitely subtle range of visual clues by which they indicated the precise function of each switch, knob and button.

The concrete hi-fi system shares none of these concerns. Its forms are anything but platonic. It is neither well mannered, nor discreet. Even today, it is still a seriously subversive, even transgressive object. You can see tangled reinforcing steel protruding from its concrete base. The heat sink emerges from the amplifier's petrified stomach like a half-digested fish supper. The vulnerability of the vinyl disc – a recording medium that was still far from obsolete at the time that the record player was designed, and of the fragile diamond-tipped stylus, make for a teeth-jarring contrast with the ragged roughness of raw concrete and rusty-looking steel. There is a surrealistic tension that comes from the knowledge that even the slightest, most gentle contact between the two would render the record useless. The deliberate exploitation of the fault line between two totally different categories of material creates a dissonance that can be compared with the impact of Meret Oppenheim's fur-lined tea cup.

There are other readings in the image of an apparently part-destroyed consumer artefact. 'Ruinist' was one word that was used to describe it at the time. This is an interpretation that Arad doesn't dispute:

'I always enjoyed watching a demolition ball in action. Part of the attraction of coming to London in the 1970s was seeing part-demolished buildings. You could still see bomb sites and re-developments with half-flattened houses revealing old wallpaper and fireplaces stacked one above the other. For me it was all new, and I took lots of pictures.'

The stereo system has echoes of those images of destruction and decay. But it was mainly the chance outcome of some casual experiments with poured concrete and electrical circuitry. Concrete was readily to hand during the building of One Off's shop in Neal Street. Just at the moment that the place was full of cement mixers, Arad met an electronics boffin.

'He could build an amplifier which was interesting, but there was something else there as well. He made me aware of what you could do with off-the-shelf audio components. I realized that hi-fi doesn't have to be contained in a box, or inside a chassis.'

The electronics needed to be waterproofed and wrapped in plastic, to be then lowered gingerly into quick-setting concrete. Along the way, there were all sorts of questions of detailed design to deal with. For example, just how were the protruding knobs to be protected from the concrete? What was the colour of the capacitors going to be – should it be selected on the basis of looking pretty – or should it simply reflect electrical engineering conventions? The concrete was carefully chiselled and fractured to ensure that it was never going to be a massive block. 'When I decided that I needed to make the turntable slightly different from a standard paving slab, I started hammering away with a chisel, just like Michelangelo.'

The response was immediate:

'I finished it, and the next week it got three pages of pictures in all the magazines. That encourages you. You learn that you can play; it taught me that I didn't have to stay exclusively in the furniture world.'

And the electronics worked, though it wasn't the quality of the sound that pulled in the customers:

'A Danish person came in and bought a stereo. It was only afterwards when he had paid for it that he asked if he could listen to it. He didn't change his mind, but he did say that he wouldn't be throwing away his B&O.'

The attention that the system attracted brought demands for more of the same. But after a lamp with a concrete base, and a small concrete table, Arad stopped. 'There was a barrage of concrete things that we could have done, but we refused. It wasn't interesting any more.'

The Concrete Stereo, 1983.
Hi-fi components encapsulated
in cast concrete. Details of the
concrete amplifier and turntable
(left) show the protruding
functioning transistors, heat
sinks etc. The concrete figures
(opposite) were cast in body-
imprinted Transformer cushions
and were prototypes for the
London Gaultier for Women shop
(see overleaf).

Bazaar, Gaultier for Women, 1986 (left). Cast concrete figures carry clothes rails on their shoulders. The Puch stool, 1981, used a ready-made, a Puch bicycle seat mounted on a wire threaded tripod base (above). The Tree Light, 1983, consisted of a concrete base containing a transformer and standard English conduit pipes and junctions with flexible goose-neck tubes and halogen lights (opposite). This handmade version was the forerunner of a standardized product now manufactured by Zeus, Italy.

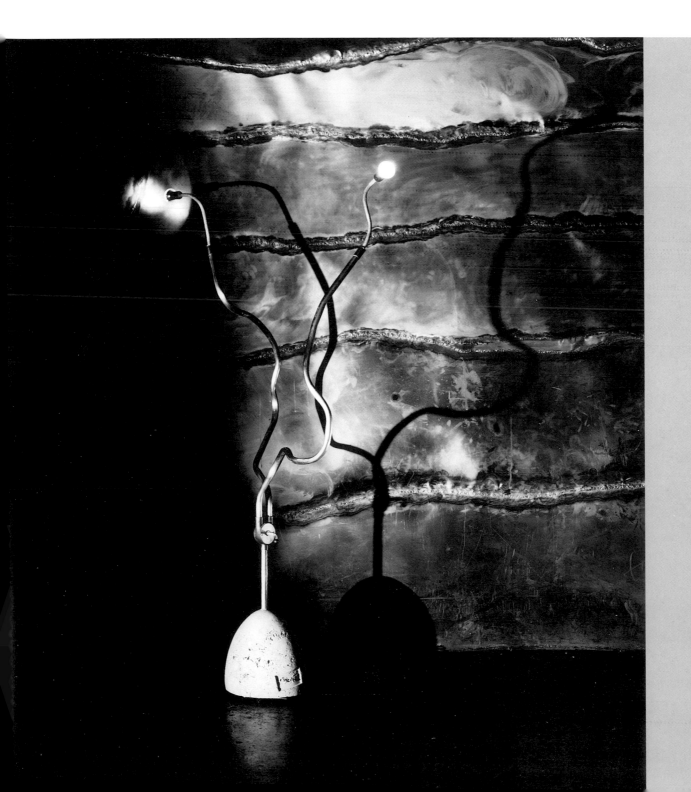

03

SHADOW OF TIME

In recent years, Covent Garden's Neal Street has been swallowed whole by London's omnivorous retail boom. In the 1980s, however, this was a marginal but lively backwater, where sandwich bars and hostels for the homeless existed cheek by jowl with artists' supply stores and cello-makers. The threat of major road building schemes kept rents low and leases short, which allowed the bright and impecunious to establish themselves here. All this has long gone: the area has now been overwhelmed by its own success, leaving chain stores to fight for dominance with street stalls peddling souvenirs.

At the start of the 1980s, Arad was able to rent a shop here from the Greater London Council which gave him a base, and a showcase for his work. It was a place in which Arad could spend time working out exactly what he wanted to be. The Kee Klamp scaffolding beds were still the mainstay of the business. And there was the chance to extend the range with a few products made by contemporaries, as well as books and magazines that customers might pick up while they were waiting. A little more success at this side of the business, and Arad might yet have turned out to be the next Terence Conran. But it was also a chance for Arad to begin exploring new directions. There was, for a start, the question of the shop itself. He was determined to transform the place, to make the most of the space, and inject into it a special quality. Given his restricted budget, there was no alternative but to make it for himself. There was a staircase to install – using concrete. And then, once this was in place, there was the requirement of the building control authorities for a handrail to prevent visitors – somewhat distracted by the musical sensors that Arad had installed in each step – from tripping over the edge.

The handrail was clearly never going to be fabricated from concrete. Part of Arad's point was to demonstrate his amusement at Building Regulations' nannyish pronouncements. But it went well beyond a prank; it proved the point of departure for Arad's continuing fascination with the creative potential of working with welded sheet steel. To the dismay of the council officials charged with enforcing the safety regulations, Arad's balustrade took the form of a swirling cone-shaped horn swooping up the stairs. The council was unimpressed and went to court to pressure Arad into doing something a little more orthodox. But the shape itself set him off on a whole series of subsequent designs that experimented with welded steel and artificial light. Here was Arad moving beyond interior architecture, and utilitarian furniture. The results were a series of objects that had what might be called a functional alibi, but which were also busily exploring the nature of objects. Out of the balustrade came Shadow of Time, a cone-shaped, irregular piece of steel, containing a light source and a clockwork mechanism that kept reasonably good time and projected a clock face on to any surface. From the same vocabulary of forms and materials came the Cone chair and the Cone table, and it was this group of objects as much as any that set Arad off on his very distinctive path through the 1980s as the most personal and original of designers.

The Shadow of Time, 1986. A working clock face is projected on to a ceiling or wall (opposite). The numbers are adjustable for focusing, and the entire top section of the volume pivots through 360 degrees. The cone form of the Shadow of Time was a development of a cone-shaped balustrade on the staircase installed by Arad in the Neal Street shop, Covent Garden (below). Railway sleepers cantilevering from a concrete wall were wired to a synthesizer so that random sounds and music were triggered by walking on the treads. The conical handrail was a later addition after attempts to retain a balustrade-free installation were overruled by a Health and Safety tribunal. It later had a second life in the Serpentine Gallery's 'Vessels' exhibition and a third as an entrance to an exhibition space within the Shelton Street studio.

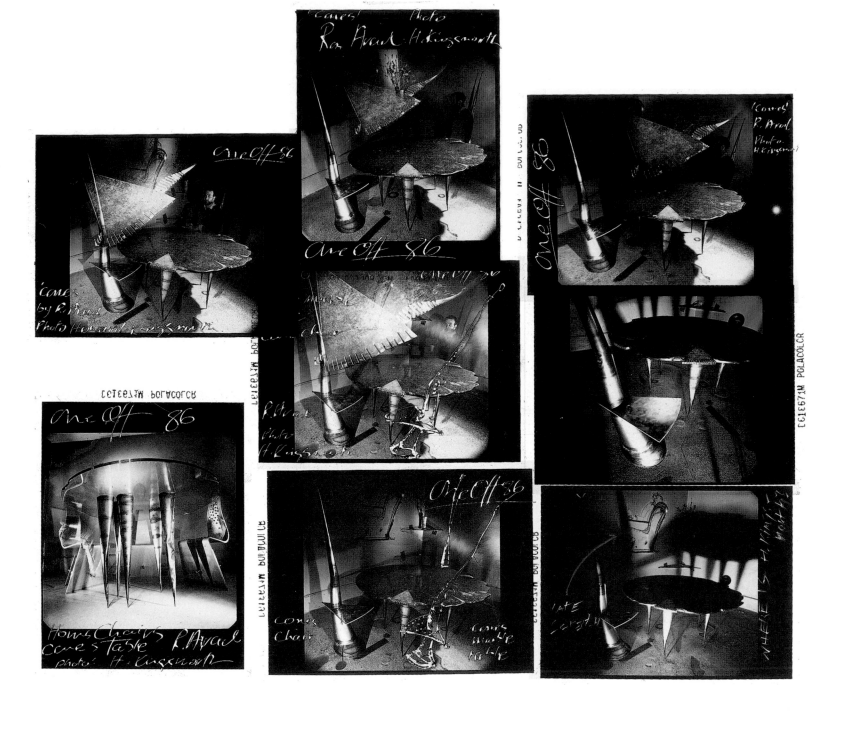

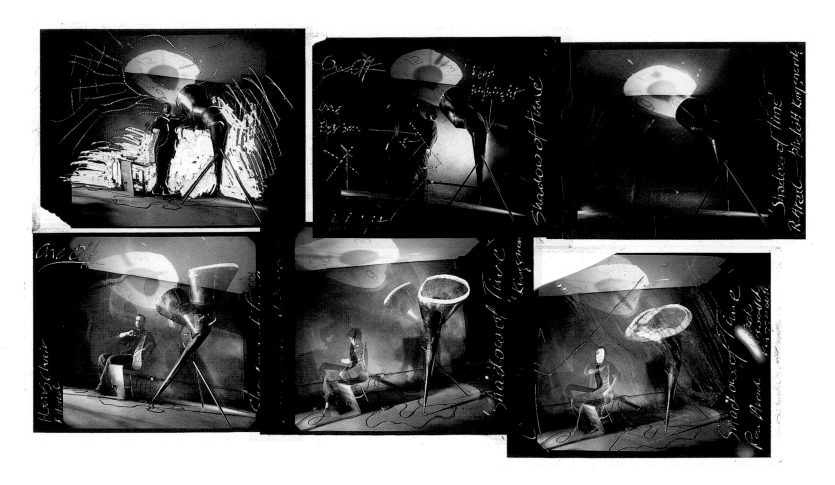

Cone tables and Horn chairs,
1985. These images were
experiments with Polaroid's
instant transparency film, the
surface of which was highly
scratchable.

04

A NEW DESCENDING STAIRCASE

When, in the early 1990s, One Off moved out of Central London to Chalk Farm, it was an important chance for Arad to use his own surroundings as the test-bed for a new creative leap – to experiment, in fact, on himself. The Chalk Farm studio – hidden from the main street, and approached through a gateway and a small courtyard – triggered an elaborate architectural project, with a swooping roof (designed with the collaboration of the engineer Neil Thomas), and a floor that swells into three-dimensional life. Both were the consolidation of a train of thought that had engaged the designer, and provided the starting point for further projects.

The same process had marked the design of the three earlier studios in which Arad had worked, in Shorts Gardens, Neal Street and Shelton Street, all within a couple of minutes' walk of each other in Covent Garden. These were not self-conscious or precious. Each of them saw Arad bubbling with energy, exploring new techniques, pouring concrete and cutting and welding metal. In each studio were architectural set pieces and technical *tours de force*. Each of them marks a new moment in the work, offering fresh directions and technical possibilities.

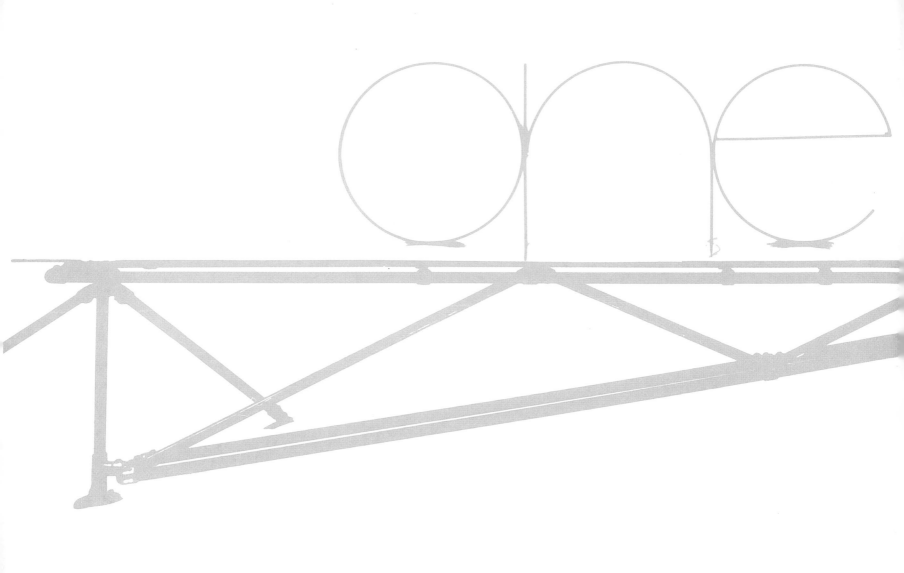

One Off, 1981 (above and left). A six-metre (20-foot) cantilevered table, pivoting across One Off's first space, formed the focal point of the potato warehouse turned showroom/work-shop.

The New Descending Staircase, 1984 (above right), installed by Arad in One Off's Neal Street showroom (see also page 25).

One Off, 1987. The raw welded
and cut steel walls of One Off's
Shelton Street space. Peepholes
at varying heights in the security
shutters allowed passers-by a
fish-eye view into the studio.

Ron Arad Associates, Chalk Farm, 1990. Calligraphic steel columns and beams support a seemingly light expanded metal ceiling and tensioned PVC roof (above right). A zig-zag of elephant-sized steps cantilevers from the steel wall, leading to a mezzanine office (below left). The main studio space seen from the undulating showroom floor (below right).

Ron Arad Associates, Chalk Farm,
1990. The studio's soft PVC windows and calligraphic columns
(opposite and above). An aerial
view of the studio (below right).

03

A WELL TEMPERED CHAIR

The first person to ask Arad to design anything with a view to manufacturing it was Rolf Fehlbaum of Vitra. Until that point, and not entirely by choice, Arad had been his own designer, manufacturer and sales force. He set himself his own briefs, he stretched his own limitations and he judged his own successes – or failures. Fehlbaum was offering the chance to do something different. Vitra was in a position not just to pay for a one-off, but to commission and manufacture a design, 'It was the first time I sat down to think "I have this commission, now what do I do?"'

This was back in 1985 – well before Fehlbaum had opened the Frank Gehry-designed chair museum at Vitra's Weil am Rhein factory, and before he had established himself as one of the most influential manufacturers in the world of workplace furniture design. Even though Vitra was little known outside Germany and Switzerland at the time, the company had a remarkable heritage of innovation, thanks to Fehlbaum's father. Its production lines turned out the full range of Eames chairs under licence from Herman Miller, and it had its own products: models of unpretentious discretion.

Fehlbaum was determined to build on this inheritance: to introduce new ranges from Mario Bellini and Antonio Citterio that would redefine the main-stream of office furniture, whilst maintaining a vigorous commitment to the cultural dimension of design. To this end, Fehlbaum conceived the idea of the Vitra Edition as a signal of his commitment to exploring new definitions of design. The edition, which included designs by Ettore Sottsass, Shiro Kuramata and Frank Gehry, had much the same relationship to the rest of Vitra's production as a Formula One racing car subsidiary to a mass-market car manufacturer. It was to serve as a test-bed for experiment and research, which might one day have a wider application. And when he talked to Arad about the project, Fehlbaum made it clear that he was looking for a design that would be free of commercial constraints.

The transition from the rough and ready One Off workshop to a highly organized and pristine factory which employed 1,100 people to make chairs provoked something of a culture shock:

'I was asked to go out to Weil am Rhein to see the factory. They could have made anything I asked them to, but when I went back to the studio, all I could design were things that I could make myself. That was the burden of having a workshop. Instead of taking advantage of the mighty Vitra, I did something that we could have done ourselves.'

That something was the Well Tempered chair. It relied not on the castings or mouldings that were inconceivable in the context of the One Off workshop with its mainly self-taught welding and bending skills, but on the simplest of formal elements, albeit with a highly challenging use of materials. With its rounded forms and squishy seat, the Well Tempered chair offers the sugges-tion of the massive solidity of a club armchair rather than its substance. Its apparent bulk is the product of a tautly curved surface, created by bending a thin sheet of flat, tempered steel just a few millimetres thick, and holding it in position with a couple of wing nuts. Assembling the chair is more like dress-making than conventional furniture production. It is made from four sheets of steel, pattern-cut to give the right shape.

Tempered steel starts life as a solid steel rod. It is flattened into sprung steel, a process known as tempering, which gives the material the special quality of having no memory. That is to say that after being bent, tempered steel will always spring back to its original flatness when the pressure is removed. It also means that bending produces a harmonious, rather than an irregular, curve. Of course, this is a material to be approached with caution, lest the fixings come loose, and whiplash across a room. The steel looks so slender and flexible that it could easily crack under pressure. Actually, it is much tougher than it looks. But that knowledge didn't stop even Arad from experiencing the occasional twinge when the chair was put to the test:

'The bravest person was Castiglioni. He just jumped on it. I was worried about him, but he just said, "It's a chair, no?". The Well Tempered chair is all skin; no bones, no fat, no muscles. It is a true case of "what you see is what you get": nothing is hidden, or covered or coated and there is nothing beyond what you see. It is the most economical way of describing a club chair: all natural curves. No child needs an explanation; they know what it is even if they would hesitate to sit on it. Although it is made of steel, it feels like sitting on a water-bed, which was an added bonus.'

Looking back in 1997, when Vitra was discussing a re-edition of the chair, Arad acknowledged that he was extremely lucky in finding precisely the right material for the purpose the first time around:

'I didn't know how difficult it is to find exactly the kind of tempered steel needed to make the chair work. It had to be the right size, and it had to be stainless. But we got there very quickly, and there was very little change between the first cardboard and paper model I did, and the finished chair. Unlike the pieces made in the workshop, it was a very short, very intense relationship. Then it goes away and you forget about it.'

The Well Tempered chair, Vitra Editions, 1986: early sketches. Vitra was the first manufacturer to commission Ron Arad to design a mass-produced chair. Arad visited the Vitra factory but rather than take advantage of the unlim-ited manufacturing resources, he retreated to the safety of Chalk Farm and prototyped a chair that could in fact have been manufac-tured in One Off's workshops. The Well Tempered chair is made from four die-cut tempered stainless steel sheets, held in tension by a series of wing nuts. The chair formed part of the Vitra Editions collection of limited production designs .

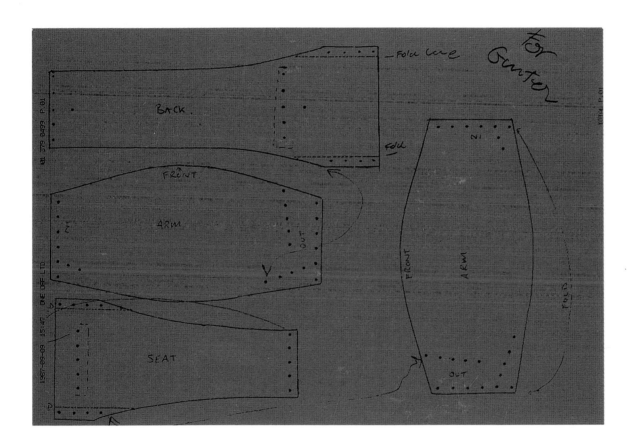

An invitation to the launch of
the Vitra Editions exhibition in
Frankfurt (above) shows the
simplicity of the patterns for the
Well Tempered chair.

06

A CONVERSATION WITH ROLF FEHLBAUM

'The first time I met Ron, he was still based in Neal Street. I went to see him, we had a drink, and we talked about Pesce and Prouvé. I was very attracted to Ron's work. It was so different from anything else that I had seen at that time. It had that "let's do it" spirit. There is an enormous vitality to it. He was able to say, "I don't need to find a manufacturer to make my work, I can invent a profession for myself." And he could do it, because he was ready to take on every stage of the process with an equal degree of obsession: design, welding, public relations, sales... Ron is really very good at all of them.

'There are really only two kinds of designer. There is the industrial designer who accepts constraints and makes as much as he can out of them. And then there is the kind of designer who is entirely driven by an idea and who spends all his effort making that idea possible. The two are very different. Some designers love constraints; they depend on them. Eames, Bellini – what they do, I love. They study problems, to which they don't have a solution, and out of that process of study and research comes their best work.

'At the other end of the spectrum is the designer who is driven by a very strong original, personal vision, with an ability to imagine an idea. These are the designers who try to make design in spite of the industrial context. Ron wants to do that. But he doesn't stand still. He is always looking to find a new kind of expression. Ron used to be completely an inventor and a maker. Now he is something different. He has become a designer who, if he isn't shaped entirely by dealing with constraints, does have a lot of understanding of them. Of course, the context has changed as well. Design as a cultural expression has become more widespread than it was, but perhaps is embraced with less enthusiasm. It is more of a profession. It has become in some ways more normal. For me, the greatest time for design is when it is linked to reform. We now have so much design, every little thing has a name. We are a little over-fed. We are interested in the anonymous, we are sick of too much bad design. We try to find the undesigned.

'Ron has the gift of surprise. He doesn't suffer solutions that live with constraints. The more you talk to a general audience, the more difficult that becomes. I wonder how far he can go and survive?'

Vitra Workshop, Germany, 1990. Before the workshop Arad asked Vitra to prepare coils of 1.5mm tempered steel, the widest available, which happened to be 30cm (11⅞in). When Arad and his team arrived they started constructing experimental pieces. The naturally harmonious curves of the tempered steel gradually transformed to controlled ergonomic shapes, providing a surprising seating sensation. Pieces made during the workshop included Beware of the Dog (opposite) and Old Dog New Tricks, Let Sleeping Dogs and Sit! (above).

Vitra chairs 1986–97. The School chair, 1986 (opposite top) was an early experiment in movement in a chair constructed out of one material. Two figures of opposing cantilevers created a swaying rather than a rocking movement. The Well Tempered chair, 1986 (opposite below) was the first Arad chair commissioned by a manufacturer. The Tom Vac chair, 1997 (above), a stacking chair with extra wide ribs, was first produced in vacuum-formed aluminium in a short run and then further developed and modified to be mass produced in injection-moulded plastic for Vitra (see page 155). The Schizzo chair, 1989 (above right), was made of veneers laminated in wide bands then sliced like salami. Arad was commissioned to design a stacking chair but the Schizzo went beyond the brief by providing two chairs in one that could be pulled apart to give two chairs from one.

07

STICKS AND STONES AND LOUIS VUITTON

Ever since it opened in 1977, the Pompidou Centre has made a commitment to design and architecture as an essential strand of its programmes, alongside art, film and music. But the appearance of design in anything but the most subordinate way, on turf conventionally seen as part of the art world, was still a novelty in the 1980s. The discourse of art has, consciously or not, developed in such a way as to make outsiders uncomfortably aware of their position as interlopers. Even when there are apparent parallels, when art and design seem to have forms in common, they have been imbued with very different meanings. An image read as art is given a very different identity from an outwardly similar object read as design.

And at the Pompidou itself, despite its ambitious embrace of inclusivity, there was precious little contact between the various sections that shared its roof. When in 1987 the design department staged its biggest exhibition on the shape of contemporary culture, as part of its tenth anniversary celebrations, it included as a stunning piece of theatre a Mirage jet fighter located in the bowels of the building, but the precise meaning of the object in a cultural sense was lost in the sheer spectacle. A Lichtenstein canvas might have conveyed the message more powerfully, but that would have been to trespass on the preserve of the Museum of Modern Art, four floors above.

This is not to doubt that the Pompidou provided a cultural context which was to have a powerful impact on some of the designers who showed their work in it. The exhibition, 'Nouvelles Tendances', brought together a number of designers from around Europe, most of them working on the borders of design and architecture, including Philippe Starck and Future Systems, as well as Arad, who were asked to produce a series of specially commissioned works. None were in the traditional model of work tailored for a design museum (following the tradition of icons in secure glass cases). Nor were they didactic demonstrations of the virtues of 'good' design. All of the schemes attempted to create specific environments: to comment on social themes, or to provide a more intense version of the designer's creative

intentions than the conventional definition of the designed object. Yet they could not really be said to have transgressed the boundaries of design. They remained in the design camp, despite Philippe Starck's attempt to launch his own version of the Happy Face logo, and Arad's knowing and playful extemporization on the language of art.

The situation was rather more complicated at the Kassel Documenta in the same year. This sprawling event has attempted to provide a portmanteau view of the fluctuating landscape of contemporary art since just after the Second World War. And this time, alongside artists of every stamp, the design world was invited as a full participant. Stefan Werwerka built a pavilion in the grounds of the city's palace. Jasper Morrison worked on what he called a global communications room. There were assorted galleries full of work by Italian and German designers, as well as exhibits by Daniel Weil and Gerry Taylor from London. The whole was presided over by Michael Ehrloff whose role had been to select the designers invited to take part.

Arad's piece was highly worked: a slab of aluminium gashed and cut, that could turn from a flat sheet into an armchair, by means of a makeshift array of hinges and cables like a mechanical magic carpet. The piece was an idea originating from the design world, but in its lack of concern for the formal conventions of manufacturing, was all about art. It was the very opposite of the highly finished 'designed' object. Rather, it was particularly raw and direct. And yet it took as its subject matter an interpretation of a theme that was of particular interest to many designers: to create an object capable of being transformed from one thing to another through a simple mechanical operation.

The reaction caught him momentarily off balance. Bruno Bischofsburger, the ayatollah of contemporary art dealers, came up and said that he wanted to buy it. 'Name a price, but I need to have your decision right away.' It was a difficult decision for Arad to make. To be bought by a dealer who represented Schnabel and Kieffer could have been a turning point for a designer who had kept a foot in the art camp. But it would also have been a burning of boats. Rolf Fehlbaum, Arad's long-standing supporter, hadn't seen the piece yet, and his continued interest had more potential in the long term than a single spark of attention from Bischofsburger. It didn't take long to say that the piece was not for sale.

Documenta confronted art and design practice and revealed just how disparate they were. One artist chose to install a rotating Mercedes saloon as a symbol of something or other. It was an act whose meaning in a conventional design exhibition would certainly have become very different, even if the same object had been installed in exactly the same way. Certainly, Documenta was not intended as a testament to the skills of the industrial designer.

In another corner there were a number of neatly crushed cubes of twisted metal that had once been cars, processed through a compactor. This was an idea that was close to Arad's earlier installation for the Pompidou, entitled Sticks and Stones – a customized metal crusher, located through the Yellow Pages, purchased from a specialist manufacturer, and suitably adorned by Arad. It sat in the Pompidou like a great growling hungry beast, waiting to be fed choice chairs that it spat out as little crushed building blocks, allowing visitors to bring their own objects to the museum and have them transformed into the installation, albeit in unrecognizable form, as part of a wall that Arad constructed with the detritus. If it was the world of art from which Rolf Fehlbaum rescued Arad by eventually acquiring the magic carpet, it was commerce that was the threat at the Pompidou. When the museum wanted to give the crusher to Louis Vuitton for a high-profile stunt to destroy counterfeit handbags, it was Fehlbaum again who stepped in to acquire the piece for the Vitra collection.

Full House, 1987. An aluminium carpet with two chairs cut into its 10mm ($^3/_8$ inch) thickness, Full House was an installation at Documenta Kassel and is now in the collection of the Vitra Design Museum, Weil am Rhein. The chairs can be winched up or folded flat to a carpet position.

Sticks and Stones, Paris, 1987.
An installation for a celebratory
exhibition to mark the Pompidou
Centre's tenth anniversary, Sticks
and Stones invited the public to
bring in their old chairs to ride
on the conveyor belt up into an
adapted car crushing machine
which then spat out compacted
boxes used as building bricks for
a wall. The exhibit was hugely
popular and many people made
several return trips.

THINGS PEOPLE DON'T REALLY NEED (BUT CAN'T AFFORD)

The landscape of contemporary culture has been shaped as much by the fault lines that fracture it, as by its increasingly few shared assumptions. Supposedly, design is not art, and art is not design. Architecture, for that matter, is neither. Which is to say that there is a gap between design, conventionally represented as being primarily concerned with pragmatic utility, and art, supposedly an activity for which cultural ambition is everything. And that gap is perceived to be unbridgeable. It is, of course, an irrational division. Who is to say that the emotional content of an object that is ostensibly a reflection of purely utilitarian concerns, such as a chair, a lamp, or a table, is less significant than that of one which has no perceived utilitarian taint? One of the most telling measures of the scale of this fiercely contested division is that of price. What, for example, is it that makes a painting by Piet Mondrian command a hundred times the value of a Red Blue chair designed and made by Gerrit Rietveld? Both are equally powerful articulations of the same particularly expressive moment in the history of culture. And yet one is the quintessence of a major art form, and the other is represented as being no more than an expression of a minor, decorative one. How could it be otherwise, when the expression of market forces is so clear? As a reflection of our wider understanding of the nature of culture, this is an issue that is of no little importance. And even more so at the level of the decisions that individuals make about their own lives. What is it that produces an 'artist', rather than a 'designer'? Is it possible to make a choice between one activity and the other, or are they inherently contradictory states of mind? For that matter, why are individuals expected to choose one camp or another, and having made that choice, to stick to it?

At art school in Israel, Arad had certainly seen himself as belonging to the art camp. Later he studied at the Architectural Association in London, where the attraction was more the city itself than the subject of his diploma: 'I was never comfortable defecting to architecture. I was a reluctant architecture student, always trying to get away with not doing what I was expected to.' Afterwards, he rapidly decided that he would rather make a precarious career designing and installing furniture than working in an architectural office. By temperament, Arad was not cut out to be anybody's assistant.

The early projects for One Off were less about designing individual objects than about the kind of problem-solving that was very much motivated by the traditional concerns of a designer.

'I never intended to become a retailer. But I needed to find an audience if I was going to be a designer. The first step was looking for a public outlet. That was exciting: sitting with lots of people, drawing bunk beds for them... trying to deal with their needs.'

The results were ingenious, but as time went by it became clear that they were still beyond the price range that the target audience of bedsit dwellers and ex-students – not so different from Arad himself – could afford. He might not be failing in terms of the quality of the objects he was making, but there was a gap between the intellectual underpinning of the project, and the reality of the way that they were put to use. The kind of people that did buy his work were more interested in the approach and the ideas, than the price. They had an appeal that went beyond simple utility.

In other words, while One Off's prices left Arad struggling to make a living, One Off's actual customers could afford to spend more. Instinctively, Arad understood that an object with the ability to take on the resonances of an artwork belonged to an entirely different economic universe from one that was intended to solve domestic problems. Here was an opportunity for the taking. The intellectual and physical effort was the same, but art that had design as its subject matter might prove a more satisfying path to follow, than attempting to carve out an even more precarious existence as a designer. 'I never said, "I'm fed up with this", but I did say to myself, "is this really what I want to do?"', says Arad of the moment in his career when he made a switch away from Kee Klamp and scaffolding and moved toward the polished welded-steel armchairs of the Volumes series.

Of course, even to try to express such a choice in words is problematic. The assumptions of contemporary culture are inevitably based on a presumption that it is impossible to make a choice between two such supposedly distinct activities, and that in some indefinable way we find ourselves irretrievably

The Big Easy, 1988. A large, hollow, welded volume with comically oversized arms, the Big Easy heralded a new direction for the London studio and spawned a large family of pieces with the same design language. The early pieces were crudely formed. The rough welds were like piping on an upholstered chair. With time, the Volumes became increasingly refined; the welds were ground and polished until they completely disappeared.

bound up with one thing or the other. But this somewhat romantic view does not in truth reflect realities. Producing artefacts that people needed, and could afford, was a losing battle. Instead, One Off moved toward what might be called 'doing things people didn't need – and selling them at a price that most people couldn't afford', as Arad self-deprecatingly puts it.

'You can't really compete with big organizations, or with real retailing. Even my affordable things were actually quite expensive. We were very price conscious, we had a sacred mark up mechanism. It was very simple: we just doubled everything. But it didn't work. The only way we got anywhere was when we broke that taboo, and accepted that things just had to cost as much as they had to cost. We discovered that we couldn't participate in the economy as it was. We had to invent another one. The good thing was that nobody else was doing it, there was no role model, and nobody to compare ourselves with. The bad point was that we didn't manage to educate enough people to relate to the things that we were making. They would buy a Picassoesque print for a lot of money, but they wouldn't spend half of that on a welded and polished steel piece. We took a decision that we shouldn't worry about the process, we just made things to see what would happen and charged what we had to. It turned out to be better to sell one piece for ten pounds, than a hundred pieces for one.'

This was the moment that welded steel entered the repertoire in an important way for the first time. The One Off workshop assumed increasing importance, and its products, while retaining the vestiges of the formal language of furniture, were clearly looking at other issues as well – a shift in focus reflected by the imposing bulk and weight of the work, and its production in limited numbers. One Off pieces became more and more expressive, less and less based on function and purpose. They weren't craft pieces, but the making of them did become an increasingly important issue.

It wasn't a move that came from nowhere. The Rover chair had to be cut and chopped, and that required a workshop. But Arad had no particular craft skills in metalwork. And making these pieces triggered a particular culture in the burgeoning One Off workshop – as Arad says, 'To polish one of these chairs is a nightmare; it became a fairly macho process.' The self-taught Arad would make the first of a series from drawings, and then the workshop members would compete with each other to make ever more complex and difficult pieces. But Arad never lost sight of the aspect of design in the objects:

'They are still chairs; it would be unsatisfactory if they weren't. There always had to be some attributes to do with sitting, and how it is to be seen sitting in one. You could say that the Volumes series is always functional, but doesn't always have to be practical. It is as heavy as it is expensive. It could be a lot lighter and a lot cheaper, but it doesn't really matter how heavy it is. It is not about lightness. Maybe some should have been heavier, perhaps even absolutely unmovable. But it is not a big panic if something becomes practical in the process. You don't always need to have an entire intellectually coherent theoretical underpinning. You don't always have to know exactly why you do something, although it helps to have an intuition, and you do need to have things to say.'

As the Volumes series matured, it went through significant changes:

'I used to think that all that welding was really good, but really it was just the best that we could do at that time, and it was quite crude. I didn't know enough to know how to get rid of the weld marks. But you make a virtue of necessity; you tell yourself that you don't want to lose the immediacy of the original drawing for a piece, and the crudeness of the way the object is put together. The welds became the memory of the drawing. It's something that you believe in at the time, at least until you discover that you can remove the welds. You look at the early Volumes, and the main thing about them is the crudeness; it's almost primitive, and you look at a later one, and you admire the seamless slickness. It's the same chair, the same limited edition, but obviously a different thing. The shift came with different resources and then different interests. There was a time when the most testing job was polishing. It sparked off a competition in the workshop to see who polished best.'

Initially, the Volumes series were made casually, as one-offs. Gradually they turned into limited editions, signed and numbered, as collectors, especially from Germany, became seriously interested. There was never a stencil, or any record of how to make the individual chairs. As a result, the similarity of an early Big Easy to a late one is smaller than that of two Giacomettis.

'It created its own sort of economy, and its own public, and it worked for us. Each time we made something, we looked at the prices we had to charge, and we asked ourselves, "Will people buy it?" They did, but the prices weren't artificial. It's not like selling splatter paint canvases for £40,000 just because you can. The prices turned out to reflect the reality, the real cost of things. The price showed the real effect of working by hand with lots of people. And it worked: it was the first time we were buoyant. It was freedom from production costs dictating everything. We never had to deal with thinking "Oh, we have this idea, but we can't do it because it's too expensive."'

The Little Heavy, 1989. A small, hollow, symmetrical volume, narrowing almost to a knife edge at the back.

The After Spring, 1992. This rocking daybed is made in mirror-polished stainless steel or in mild steel. The double-skinned base contains a lead ballast and this concealed weight gives a surprisingly balanced movement. The tapering 'wings' are 'boned' with sprung steel. Size 10, 1988 (opposite) is a hollow armchair, so-called because it requires that the sitter is no larger than a UK size 10.

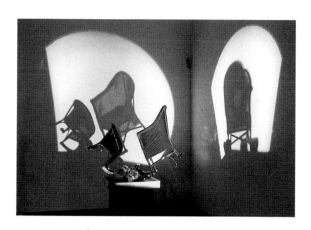

The Rolling Volume, 1989 (opposite) is a large rocking armchair weighted in its base to provide a surprising balance. This piece has evolved over the years, at first having parallel sides and later tapering to a single line at the back. The first Rolling Volume, produced in 1988 (above right), was weighted with free-flowing sand to allow the balance of the chair to shift to suit the weight of the sitter. Looming Lloyd, 1989 (top right), is an original Lloyd Loom chair with its front legs mounted on extremely heavy elongated feet (weighing approximately 100 kilograms/221 pounds), allowing the back legs to be suspended in the air when the chair was not in use. Spanish Made, 1990 (top left) is a polished, welded chair heavily weighted to the front. The weight of the sitter forces the chair back to its traditional position. The chair was so-named because it was first made during a workshop in Spain.

Italian Fish, 1988 (above) takes
its name from a chair designed for
the Italian manufacturer Cassina
by Gaetano Pesce, to which
Arad's piece bears a vague
similarity. 2Rnot, 1992 (opposite)
is a blackened volume from which
chairs of various heights are
excavated. Four positions of
the six-sided cube are chairs,
while two are not. The cuts
are 'repaired' with polished
stainless steel.

Narrow Papardelle, 1992 (opposite) consists of a long flexible strip of polished, woven stainless steel, similar to that developed for conveyor belts in the food industry. The first three metres of the strip are welded on to steel side profiles, and the remaining three can flex and roll, forming a carpet extension or a rolled-up footrest. Eight By One, 1991 (above) is a series of three different cantilevered chairs, each made from internally sprung steel strips, 2.4 metres (eight feet) long and 31 centimetres (one foot) wide.

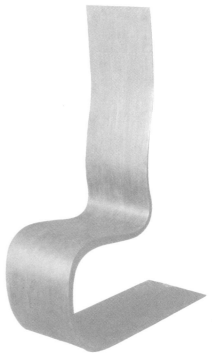

0360

FROM UDINE TO BOLOGNA AND BACK AGAIN

The design-led, family-owned firm is one of the most distinctive features of Italian industry. It is a phenomenon that is often cited as being in large measure responsible for the success of a medium-sized tier of business that simply doesn't exist in Britain or America. Certainly, these firms are a reflection of the enthusiasm with which Italians established their industrial culture in the post-war years. Because they reflect the personal engagement of owner-managers, they have taken it for granted that design is an issue that matters. Such people have taken pride in producing beautiful, charismatic objects. It is an inherited pride, not something that has been driven home by state-sponsored propaganda.

The same pattern has repeated itself time and again: the success of the founding generation is based on traditional workshop skills – leather, woodwork or metal. Those skills have been put to work by the second generation using the language of contemporary design. The most critical moment is often when the third generation has moved into the driving seat. Sometimes, as in the case of Alessi, it allows for a new bout of experimentation to flourish. Sometimes it sees the original spark being lost. But for better or worse, family ownership has allowed companies to pursue personal passions and enthusiasms, rather than answer to the conventional wisdoms of shareholders and investment analysts. It is both an enviable phenomenon, and one which has not been without its occasional problems. While most companies have seen it as their responsibility to put fresh investment into the business, every so often there has been a Zanussi that has put its entire existence at risk by ploughing every available lira into acquiring costly new players for the local football team.

For such businesses, and for the Italian furniture world in general, the early 1990s were a difficult period. Italian designers no longer seemed to have the same effortless command of the agenda that they had enjoyed, almost since the end of the 1950s. Between them Sottsass and Castiglioni, Bellini and Magistretti, Branzi and Mendini had dominated the terms of the debate on design. But after the Memphis explosion of the mid-1980s, that effortless grip had faltered. At the same time, some of the major Italian manufacturers were finding themselves on the economic defensive. Some, such as Cassina, were acquired from their original owners by multinationals. Others, such as Arflex, vanished altogether.

Such is the background to Arad's relationship with Moroso, a family-run firm based in Udine, a remote north-eastern part of the country. Arad began to work with them at the point at which the company was going through a generational transition, with creative direction coming from a younger daughter, newly returned from university in Bologna. Until this point, Moroso had been a relatively low-profile company, with solid, well-made products, content to leave the pioneering to others. In the course of three years however, all this changed, with a series of commissions – Arad's among them – to a younger generation of designers. For Arad this was almost his first commission from a mainstream company, where the point of the exercise was to come up with a commercially successful design, rather than produce a piece of attention-grabbing image-building. The result was a number of pieces of upholstery that translated the forms of the metalwork that was engaging the One Off studio into affordable, domesticated products.

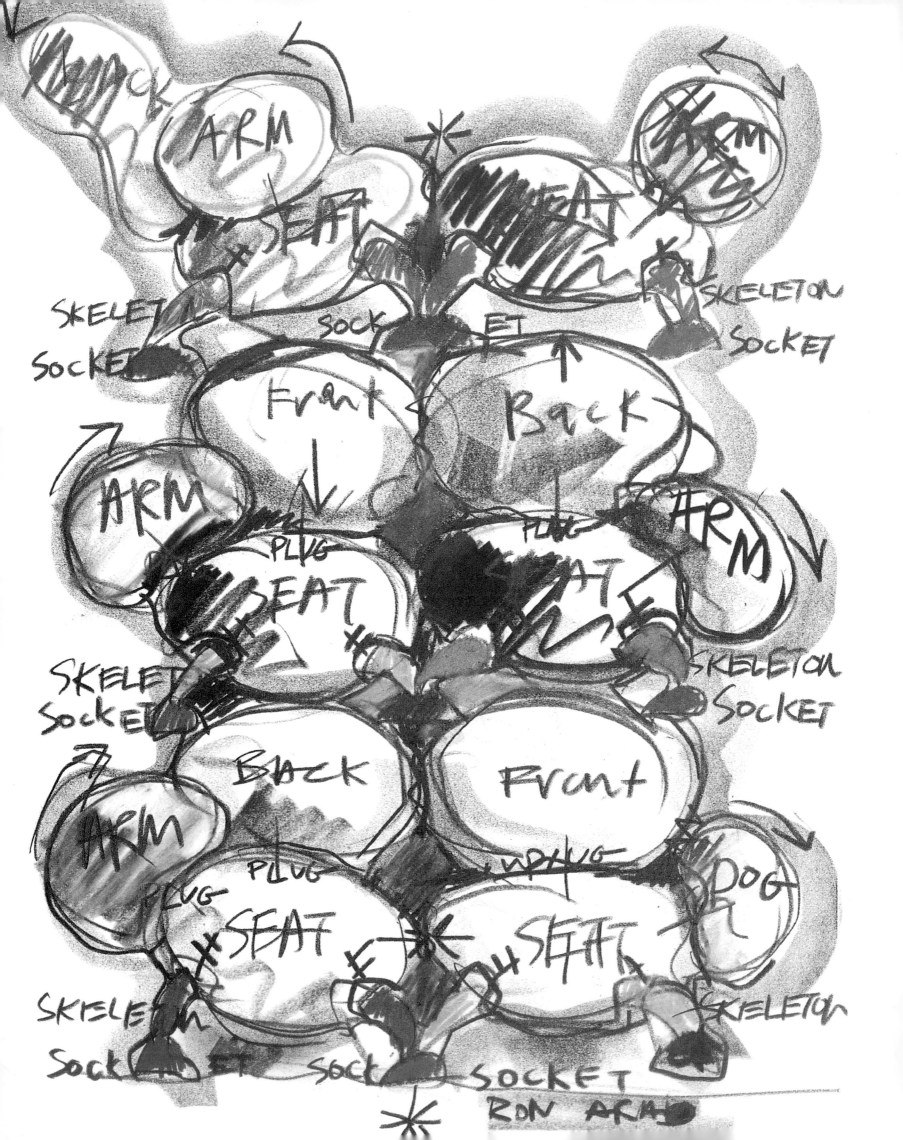

Sof-Sofs, Moroso, 1995. This modular seating system has slot-on multi-position arm- and backrests. Individual seats and footrests connect to one another via the domed feet, allowing an unlimited number of units to be joined and curved as required.

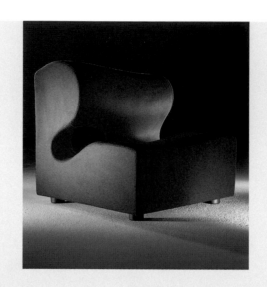

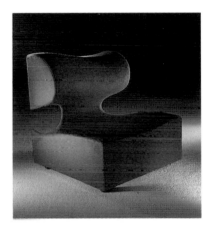

Misfits, Moroso, 1993. A mock modular upholstered system, Misfits was designed for the launch of the ICI material Waterlily, an eco-friendly water-blown foam. Each of the four sections was carved from a 90cm (35¹/₂in) Waterlily cube. The idea was to produce a set that looked deliberately mis-registered. The result was a family of pieces that appeared to have been cut out of a bigger landscape and then rearranged.

The Spring Collection, Moroso,
1990. This comprised ten
different upholstered chairs,
many of the shapes being direct
translations from the metal
originals.

5 to 10

STEFANO'S BAR

It is 1992, a few weeks before the opening of the Milan Furniture Fair. The One Off studio is working at full tilt. Making a big show on the annual fringe in Milan has become a tradition for Arad – a chance not just for useful exposure and networking, but also to help pay the bills for the year ahead by selling the latest collection to the flying circus of gallery owners, museums, dealers and enthusiasts attracted by the event. It is a gruelling process both physically and creatively. Milan is a circus, a fish bowl and a rumour mill, in which you are only as good as your last magazine cover. The pressure to come up with something fresh, attention grabbing, and at the same time credible has never been more intense. In the last decade the increasingly jaded audience has devoured – and spat out again – half a dozen movements, from Memphis to Minimalism.

The pressure to do it all against the shipping deadlines, and to actually produce high-quality artefacts is – or was – all but intolerable, especially for Arad, who combines a flair for showmanship with a sharp sense of self-criticism. Into this pressure cooker atmosphere walks a distraction: an Italian businessman, Stefano Ronchetti. He wants a bar designed for a site in Milan, and he wants it in a hurry. Arad has more pressing matters in mind. But Ronchetti comes with an introduction from an old friend, Davide Mercatali – the man who started the Milanese group Zeus, and who was responsible for giving Arad his first exhibition in the city. So Arad listens.

'Ronchetti said, "Please could we work on the project?". I didn't want to say no, just like that, so we thought about what we reckoned would be an impossible price for the job, and doubled it. He said, "I need to think," went off for a walk, came back, and said "Yes."'

Arad was still not disposed to treat the project as anything other than a chore.

'We said to ourselves, "OK. We will do something so difficult that they'll wish they had never asked us." We were so arrogant – we thought we were the first people ever to polish metal.'

What Arad did not know about Ronchetti's business was that it had at its heart an extremely accomplished sheet-metal fabrication workshop. It is a typical example of that north Italian phenomenon; the family-led, medium-sized firm with a special expertise in manufacturing. From its base in Cantu – on the outer fringe of the Milan conurbation – Ronchetti was able to plug into the network of similar firms that are jointly responsible for the best of Italian manufacturing. These are to design what the Silicon Valley companies once were to computers. Ronchetti specializes in metal fabrication. Down the road is another firm with unmatched expertise in wood, and in the next village are a couple of injection moulders. Together, they were more than capable of dealing with anything that Arad could throw at them.

The bar design was a swirling set of highly polished interlocking curved surfaces which would have been extraordinarily difficult to make in the One Off studio. It belonged to the family of Arad's work at the time, and had a marked resemblance to the bar that he would go on to design for the Belgo Noord restaurant in London. The reflective curves had a curious insubstantiality – as if they had been airbrushed, or even Photoshopped into existence. But as soon as the drawings had been dispatched to Cantu, Arad promptly put all thought of the job out of his mind.

'We almost forgot about it: we went to see it after our own [Milan Fair] private view at the Facsimile Gallery. And it was almost embarrassingly well done. It was like Charlie Chaplin going to a look-alike contest, and coming in second. They had done it better than we could.'

Such was the uneasy beginning of what has turned out to be one of the most significant developments in Arad's career, the start of a continuing relationship that has led to the closure of the One Off workshop, and its translation into a conventional design studio with Ronchetti's factory taking over the role that the workshop used to play.

The relationship took some time to consummate. After the unexpected success of the bar project, Ronchetti became involved in a series of subsequent collaborations with Arad. Sometime before, Arad had been involved with a project organized by Borek Sípek, working with the Dutch company Artifort – it was what Arad called 'a blind date with an idea', involving different

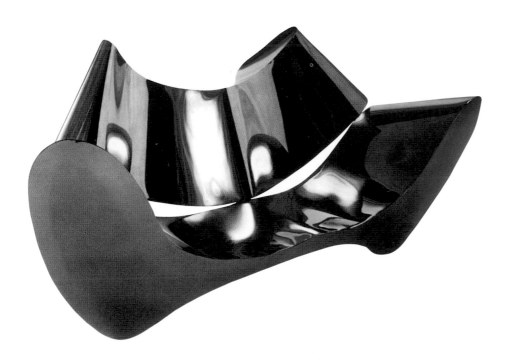

attempts to package or create boxes for existing generic pieces of furniture. Somehow the project never came to fruition at the time. But on the strength of their performance in Milan, Arad looked again at the possibility of making the pieces, this time with the cooperation of Ronchetti. And this led to the beautifully engineered Box in Four Movements, with its dependence on a set of carefully calibrated springs, as well as And The Rabbit Speaks and A Suitable Case, which formed the basis for Arad's first post-Ronchetti exhibition, focused around boxes. It transformed Arad's working methods; the One Off studio was limited to working in steel. Ronchetti could work aluminium with equal ease, and could pull in its neighbours to help on anything else.

'They would shout a lot, but then they would work out a way to make just about anything,' remembers Arad, who grew increasingly delighted at the possibilities that an association with Ronchetti allowed. It removed the drudgery, it transformed the economics, and it allowed him to look at technically far more challenging projects. It led him finally to close the work-

shop in 1992, and sign an agreement with Ronchetti to make the One Off studio pieces.

The decisive moment was the commission for the Opera House in Tel Aviv (see page 87).

'We went to an English company, who looked at the project for a month and then said, "Sorry, it's a little over our heads." Ronchetti were then invited to tender for the project. When they came and took a look at what we were doing, they couldn't believe what they saw: all these art school graduates cutting metal and killing themselves in the process. "Ron, why don't we do it for you?", they asked, and of course, they were right. There might have been a few disappointed German collectors who seemed to want to have my actual blood on the pieces they bought. But our capacity didn't just double, it was endless, and we could begin to assume that everything would be well-made and would work.'

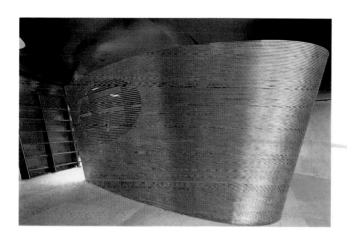

Spazio Metals bar, Milan, 1992 (opposite top). Executed in mild steel and stainless polished steel, this was the first volume piece not to be made in the One Off London workshop. When Marzorati Ronchetti, Italy, approached Arad to commission a stainless steel bar, he was too busy preparing for the Milan show and initially tried to put them off by showing them

drawings of something that would be too difficult to make. Unknown to Arad, however, Ronchetti owned one of the best steel fabrication workshops in Italy. When Arad saw the finished bar he was so impressed by its quality that he subsequently invited them to take over One Off's steel production when the London workshops closed. The **St.St. sofa, 1994** (opposite

bottom) was the last piece made in London before the One Off studio ceased production. Made for Draenert Studio, Germany, the sofa has a seat and back that only touch at three points. The three-dimensional weld points make it even stronger. The bronze wall and the amphitheatre stairs of the **Tel Aviv Opera House, 1994** (above and right) were made by Marzorati Ronchetti.

Fly on the Wall, 1994 (opposite and above right) is a shelving system that folds out of a 30x30x30cm (11⁷/₈in) cube. Produced in bronze, steel or wood, its configuration can be different on each installation. **Box in Four Movements, 1994 (above)** is a 40x40x40cm (15³/₈in) box in four sections with three of the sections adjustable to any height or angle. Ratchet joints allow exact fixing. Despite looking hard-edged, the sections were hinged on a torsion bar, giving the chair a subtle bouncy comfort. The original complicated ratchet mechanism was later simplified: the adjustment can now be made with an electric screwdriver. Castors make the piece easy to move but lock when the chair is occupied.

The aluminium box/case
And The Rabbit Speaks, 1994
(below) is a chair in its own right,
but on opening it up two Vitra
Edition Schizzo chairs emerge.
A Suitable Case, 1994 (opposite)
is a lockable cherrywood ply case
which holds one Papardelle chair.
The case itself is also a chair.

Belgo Noord, London, 1993. When a Belgian restaurant opened close to the Chalk Farm office, Arad and his team started to go there regularly for lunch. As the interior was so similar in style to One Off, many people assumed Arad had designed it. When Belgo later decided to convert an adjacent courtyard they commissioned Ron Arad Associates to design the extension. RAA designed it so that the outdoor feel was preserved. Giant steel and wood double-edged fins provided the structure to hold glass roof panels, at the same time creating a brise-soleil. Marzorati Ronchetti provided all the more demanding elements such as the bar (above and right). Belgo Noord was followed in 1995 by Belgo Centraal, a much larger restaurant in Covent Garden with an interior designed by RAA.

The Domus Totem, Milan, 1997.
This ambitious installation was
constructed by Marzorati
Ronchetti (see page 153).

11

FITZCARRALDO

Arad had been designing for almost ten years before a serious architectural project materialized. And even then, it wasn't a free-standing building. What was on offer, after an informal selection process that involved Gae Aulenti, Mario Bellini and Hans Hollein, was the chance to plant a cuckoo in the nest. Tel Aviv's Opera House is one of Israel's most ambitious cultural projects. Its architect, Jacov Rechter, was looking for a designer who could shape the public spaces in a way that would reflect that ambition without impinging on his own work. Uneasy brief though it might have been, this was a much more important and challenging project than it sounded, and was to dominate the studio's thinking for much of the protracted development period that it took to transform the original idea into reality.

The Opera House was itself the product of many years of planning. It was intended to form a new urban focus for Tel Aviv, a city that is the hybrid product of a planning regime that confronts principles derived from the English welfare state with the North American market economy, a confrontation which in turn is overlaid on an ancient landscape. Rechter's building forms part of a complex that faces the Israeli defence ministry across one of the city's major thoroughfares. It includes a museum built in the 1960s, as well as a library and offices. The Opera House has a formal entrance, located well away from the traffic through an expansive glass entrance wall which is approached from a new pedestrian square. The building itself is characterized by the extensive use of biscuit-coloured stone: in terms of architectural quality, it is uneven, making several attempts at grand gestures with an uncertain vocabulary.

The main issue for the interior was not so much to decorate the foyers – to select furniture, colours, finishes and light fittings – but to create a sense of place, to design the spaces in which opera-goers could relax during the interval, have a drink, eat a meal, buy a book or leave their coats. The European opera house has always been a place in which the musical and functional requirements of the auditorium have been accompanied by a series of grand social spaces in which a city's élite can engage in public life. And they form an aspect of the opera that is as important as its ostensible function. Tel Aviv follows precisely this model, even if Arad's spaces are as

challenging as the most demanding of contemporary music. The approach was to use the Opera's foyer as the landscape in which to construct a number of free-standing objects that related and played off each other, more than they related to their host. It wasn't that they ignored their setting, but there could never be any doubt, even to the most casual glance, that they were not part of it, that they represented a quite different attitude.

The first response to the project was the purchase of a powerful computer-aided design system, apparently a casual decision, but one that was eventually to have an important impact on Arad's work, in entirely unexpected ways. This was at a moment when even the largest high-tech architectural practices were still designing with Rapidographs. Unfortunately, the team at Arad's studio were never quite able to master the system's complexities: 'We had the computer but we had nobody who could operate it.' The resulting wire diagram renderings seemed pretty impressive at the time however, especially since they came from a studio that looked like a rusty steel cave, and from a designer who was principally associated with the use of the welding torch. But for all the effort, the CAD drawings didn't ever quite manage to describe the entire project:

'It was like buying a grand piano, a score and a set of instructions on how to use the keys, and hoping for the best. It took us a week to plot out an A3 page, and the computer would keep crashing. We were very happy with even a half-complete drawing. Luckily, the machine was stolen.'

It didn't matter too much since the Tel Aviv project was postponed for a year. When it came to life again, Arad had moved studios and shifted gear. Computing power had become cheaper and easier to handle. But there was still no rush to use it. The design of the Opera foyers was carried out over countless carefully, even obsessively delineated hand drawings by a constantly changing cast of collaborators. Funding came and went, reflecting an uncertain political and economic climate. What had seemed like a modestly scaled, but demanding project was taking on the qualities of an epic, involving constant travel by the design team, and a concerted effort to

realize the free-flowing forms of the scheme. There was a hugely ambitious attempt to bring the refined fabrication and detailing of European high design to the intellectually no less sophisticated context of the Middle East, in which the delicate touch of advanced construction technique was conspicuous mainly by its absence. Small wonder then that the project at times appeared to be taking on the qualities of Werner Herzog's film *Fitzcarraldo*, with its quixotic attempts to drag a paddle-steamer across the rivers and mountains of Amazonia.

The epic scale of the undertaking was represented mainly on paper, through an enormous number of drawings. And what drawings they were, full of energy and emotional force. Until the Opera House was finally completed, it was never quite clear what Arad's project would be like: his heavy black pencil sketches showed sweeping Möbius strip curves that defied conventional interpretation. They showed steps and curves and complex shell geometries that gave a hint of an aesthetic universe entirely removed from the orthogonal nature of Rechter's grid. The drawings in themselves had a remarkable power.

What made possible the transformation of the drawings into reality was the dedication of the site engineer, and the relationship that Arad had previously established with Ronchetti, the Italian subcontractor responsible for the metalwork involved in his designs. It was a transformation that paved the way to a new stage in Arad's career, allowing him to move beyond the widely held impression of him as exclusively a maker. One of the constants of Arad's approach to design is his belief in the improvisational, in demanding the freedom to change his mind continually during the process. In the early part of his career that freedom came from the workshop, which allowed him the space to turn half-formulated ideas into finished forms through a process of trial and discovery. The Opera House was a point of

The Tel Aviv Opera House Foyer, 1994. The underbelly of the auditorium is perforated with cavities to accommodate both monitors for latecomers and lighting elements. The wall is constructed from rods of bronze and provides areas of seating within its form. The sprayed concrete 'island' in the foyer contains the kitchens, bars and restaurant.

transition. It was fabricated by Ronchetti in Italy, rather than by One Off in London and it was installed by contractors more than by Arad himself. The possibility of freedom, of continually changing and exploring solutions, ran the risk of being eliminated from the loop. The complexities of designing in London, fabrication in Italy and site installation in Israel didn't allow for much in the way of ambiguity. Nor did a range of materials and finishes that included sheet metal, bronze tubing, as well as double-curved plaster. In this context, after the long drawn-out process of design, tendering and installation, the sense of freedom could only be smuggled in at the last minute – when Ingo Maurer arrived to install his lighting system, when the last details of the interior were put in place and when the graphic designer Neville Brody installed an enigmatic signage system. But as things turned out, the ill-fated purchase of that first computer drafting system pointed the way to an alternative means of re-introducing the uncertainty and freedom that was meat and drink to Arad. It opened the way in subsequent projects to the incorporation of computerized systems which allowed for endless exploration, through the phenomenon of designing on screen which Brody once described as 'electronic paint which never dries'.

But in the detailed design of the opera foyers, all that was still to come: 'The production manager at Ronchetti took the opera drawings and said to his boss, "See what you can do with the computer?". But of course, the drawings weren't actually done on computers. It is inconceivable now to think that the drawings could have been done in the way they were. I was in danger of being left out of the computer revolution.'

When the Opera House was under construction, technology was not that sophisticated, but nevertheless a virtual model of the project was assembled:

'What seemed amazing then was just a primitive walk-through that looks really old-fashioned now. But it was the first time we could "see" the Opera, and we lived with that image, and clung to it like a religious icon: it helped get us through.'

It wasn't the only chance that Arad got to reassure himself that he was on the right track with the Opera House design. During the last stages of the

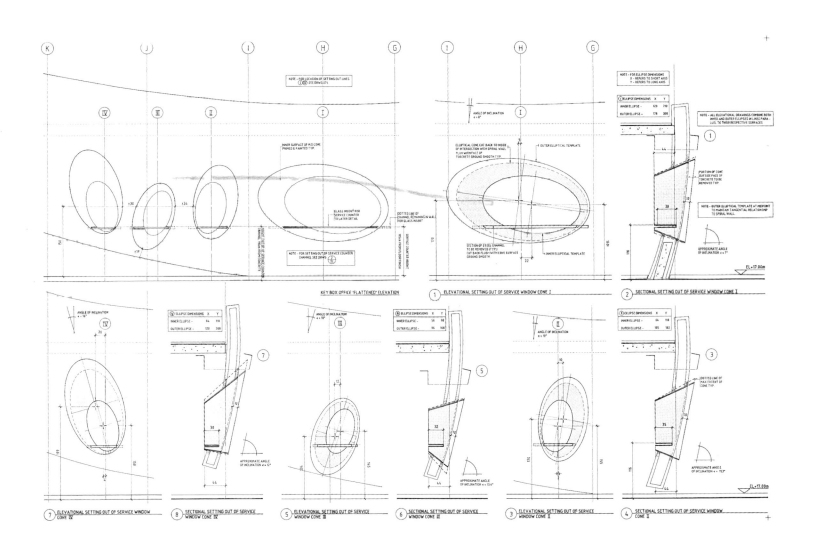

The island under construction (opposite). The metal becomes the shuttering that defines the ovals during the concrete spraying. Working drawings of the island and box office windows (above).

Opera House, he completed a small clothing shop in Milan, Michelle ma Belle, which served as a kind of test-bed: 'The Opera building had already been designed, the shop tried some of the same forms, but we had never seen the white curved walls with holes, and saw how it looked in an "arte povera" version. In the Opera there was a process of obsessive drawing that left nothing for interpretation. Michelle ma Belle was looser.'

But the Opera House was an entirely new direction. It was a one-off, a design that represented new ground, both in terms of form and materials. When the Israeli premier eventually presided over the opening ceremonies for the new building, he gave his country an architectural experience that represented a completely fresh departure. Inside the stolid frame of reference of the stone and glass of the Opera House itself, the elements of the foyer ricochet, seemingly at impossible speed, back and forth like the fragments left by an explosion. The sinuous streamlined forms express a great burst of energy within a building that otherwise seems half asleep. Within Rechter's building, Arad's work is an attempt to explore a world of design and materials that is challenging and original. There is nothing else quite like it.

The Opera House box office. The window (above) was in fact installed upside down by the constructors but was allowed to remain like this.

HORIZONTAL SECTION THRU
AUDITORIUM SOFFIT

LINE OF AUDITORIUM
CLADDING ABOVE

CRUSH BAR
BELOW.

MEZZ
BAR

AMPHI/STAIRS

ART GALLERY
BY OTHERS

CONICAL
OPENING

BRIDGE

CONICAL
OPENING

015

021

A bronze staircase leads to
the mezzanine level of the
island which doubles as an
amphitheatre for an audience
of a hundred during foyer
performances. The plans for
setting up the amphitheatre show
how the free-form outlines of the
stairs fan out from a focal point.

The bookshop window in the
bronze wall. The window was
created by removing every other
bronze rod.

The view into the bookshop (above) with a lighting 'egg' above. The heavy door to the bookshop pivots on one socket in the concrete floor. Depending on whether it is open or closed, it totally changes the appearance of the shop (below).

An early model for one of the long, meandering bars (below). Computer image of the island (opposite). Arad convinced the client to invest in building the virtual model. For the architectural team this was almost a religious symbol during the four years of the design process.

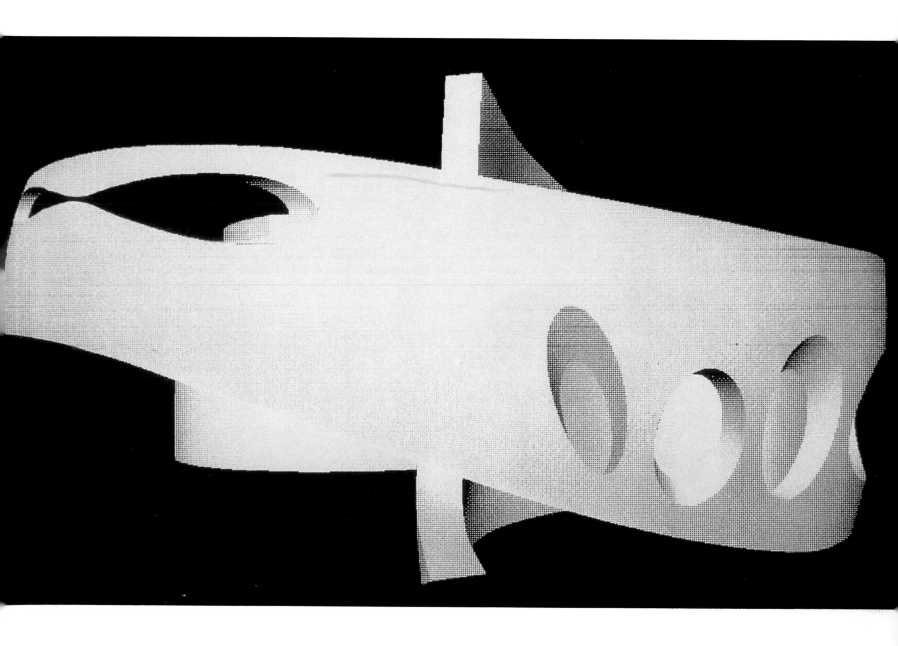

window
mannequins

interior elevation left

to changing
room

mirror

counter

interior elevation night.

customer

window

mannequin

Michelle ma Belle, a shop in Via
della Spiga, Milan, 1993. This
interior, designed while the
Opera House Foyer was being
conceived, involved the
experimental use of free-form
shapes in sprayed concrete.

THE HELICOPTER DISAPPEARED INTO THE SKY TOWING THE PIPE OUT OF THE FACTORY WHILST THE MACHINE WAS STILL EXTRUDING IT

To use a fashion analogy, the Bookworm – Arad's best-selling shelving system for Kartell – was his first excursion into the ready-to-wear market. After two very successful decades of making nothing but couture clothes, here was a product that had something for everyone. After concentrating on the workshop, and on producing limited editions of painstakingly hand-crafted metal objects, here was a factory-made product extruded from plastic and that sold by the kilometre rather than the metre. You could take the result home in a carrier bag, screw it to the wall, and load it with your paperbacks all in the course of a single afternoon.

Instead of making Arad's work the currency of the gallery and museum system complete with certificates of authenticity, Kartell had manufactured a piece that was genuinely accessible for the first time – if not quite in every high street, then certainly in every city. All this was made possible thanks to a new approach to manufacturing. Kartell was no longer an old-style manufacturer with a factory of its own, producing its products under its own roof, as it once had been. Under new ownership, it relied on subcontracting – it financed and owned the tooling needed to make a product, but it didn't make products itself. Kartell found the most appropriate subcontractor for the job, and as a result, it could engineer a product to a specific price. The outcome was an Arad design that was, for the first time, available on demand from a shop. Of course, to make it all possible, an investment in tooling and marketing far beyond Arad's own resources was called for.

As analogies go, it is more revealing for the paradoxical differences between design and fashion, than for the similarities that it spotlights. For a couturier to put their name to a mass-produced product is a process conventionally presented as being cynically exploitative: a matter of a mass-produced camera, selected from an existing inventory of parts and decorated with a clichéd couturier's signature in the hope of attracting a premium price, rather than a genuine exercise in creative intelligence. But for a designer, the driving impulse of twentieth-century industrial culture has always been to measure success in terms of mass-production, rather than at the level of the one-off. And this is what the Kartell project allowed Arad to achieve for the first time. There had been other attempts to do the same thing, with Driade and Moroso for example, but the Kartell project, almost by accident, produced an unquestionably successful volume-product. The Bookworm was a chance not to charge a premium, but to make a product accessible. It was the kind of artefact that could be seen as the consummation of a designer's career, rather than merely a diversion. It was design more than it was art. And the result was something that lots of people actually wanted to buy, not because it carried the Arad signature, but because it was a fresh and original way of putting up shelves.

At the same time, this success underlines one of the more remarkable aspects of Arad's work until this point. That is, just how central a figure he had made himself, without actually engaging in the day-to-day practice of design. It is as if – to deploy yet another analogy – Hollywood had embraced as a central figure a video artist who had never made a film for commercial distribution through the studio system. And then that video-maker, twenty years into his career, had suddenly worked as a mainstream director to make a box office hit without losing the essence of the creative impulse that had sustained him until that point. From the moment that the Bookworm was launched, Arad's work was no longer on the margins of mass-production, but at its heart. That transformation allowed him to turn his earlier preoccupations into the mainstream of design without abandoning his previous convictions. The forms and the ideas he had engaged with were initially the basis for an ingenious substitute for the economics of mass-production, with the notion of producing handmade objects that were as close as possible to the language of industrial design. Subsequently they became the starting point for a form of creative expression which had its own validity, without referring to industrial design. And then finally, the aesthetic was realized within the resources of mass-production. Arad's work became 'design' in the sense that the industrial system would understand it.

This Mortal Coil, 1993. A free-
standing tempered steel spiral
bookcase, This Mortal Coil flexes,
sways and distorts under the
weight of books.

The process had a significant effect on the potential of design. It was a kind of autobiography: what Arad had done in his own studio helped to consolidate the debate on the nature of design. The compromises and diversions of one-off explorations had shaped a new view of mass-produced design. And in turn, it shaped design itself. The Kartell Bookworm had its origins in the form of a costly and technically demanding metal wall storage piece. It was a one-off, a piece of coiled, sculptural steel that undulated across an entire wall. It was as much an installation as it was a means to store a collection of books. But to install it as a product made from steel required a team of at least six people, and lots of shouting and screaming in the process. Putting it on a wall without the greatest care could lead to disaster: the original steel Bookworm could, theoretically at least, detach

itself from the wall and whiplash across an entire room. Steel is in fact very potent: the challenge was to tame the physical impact, without diminishing the idea. From the original concept of what might be called an 'art' piece, the Arad workshop produced a smaller, slightly more user-friendly version. They also created the industrial Bookworm, with a profile that was almost as thin as a razor-blade.

According to Arad, the product was 'something we knew had mileage. The original idea spawned a whole family of designs – the Mortal Coil, the Mini-Bookworm, One Way or Another, and then Lovely Rita. But the price tags of up to £11,000 seemed a bit too high for the designs to have real commercial potential. The results were still saleable, but in 1996, Kartell sold

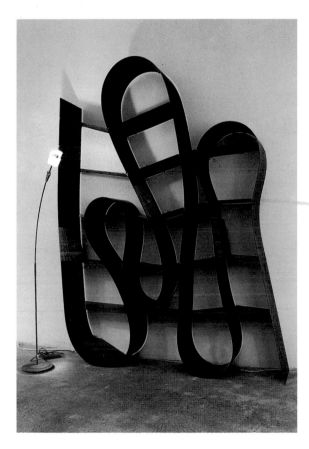
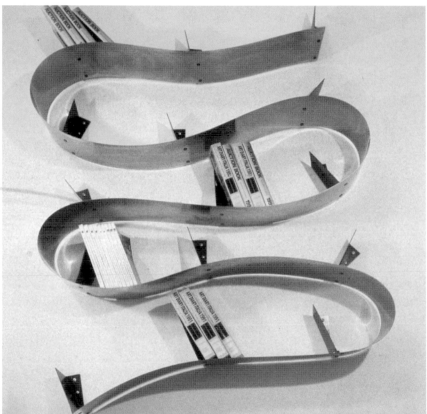

One Way or Another, 1993 (above). Named by Arad's daughter, this sprung steel bookcase was so-called due to its tendency to sway from left to right. The Mini-Bookworm, 1993 (above right) was produced as an attempt to make the product accessible to a wider market. It was made from a thinner sprung steel with small winged brackets in place of welded steel box brackets.

something like 1,000 kilometres (621 miles) of extruded plastic Bookworms, while the studio version in springy steel had sold a mere 100 metres (328 feet). Initially at least, Kartell didn't see the large-scale potential for the product. Their interest was to involve themselves in a high-profile project that would attract attention, without necessarily providing a big commercial pay-off.

'They put it into the Milan Fair to see the response. We showed a mock-up, in which the brackets were still solid. The result was an avalanche of orders. Here was a mass-produced system that could be acquired in short, cheap lengths and put together in any configuration the purchaser chose. More to the point, here was a shelving system that for the first time shrugged off the tyranny of the straight line.'

The shelving, even in short lengths, took on a powerful form, swirling across a wall like calligraphy, and could always be tailored to suit a particular requirement. No two of the installations were the same. Each could be tailored to the precise dimensions of a space. In the process of bringing the product to market, Arad had migrated from the periphery to the centre stage of the design world.

The Bookworm for Kartell, 1994. Produced in translucent plastic in a variety of colours, this was the first product designed by Arad with both mass appeal and mass affordability. It fast became Kartell's best-selling product, its success measured in kilometres.

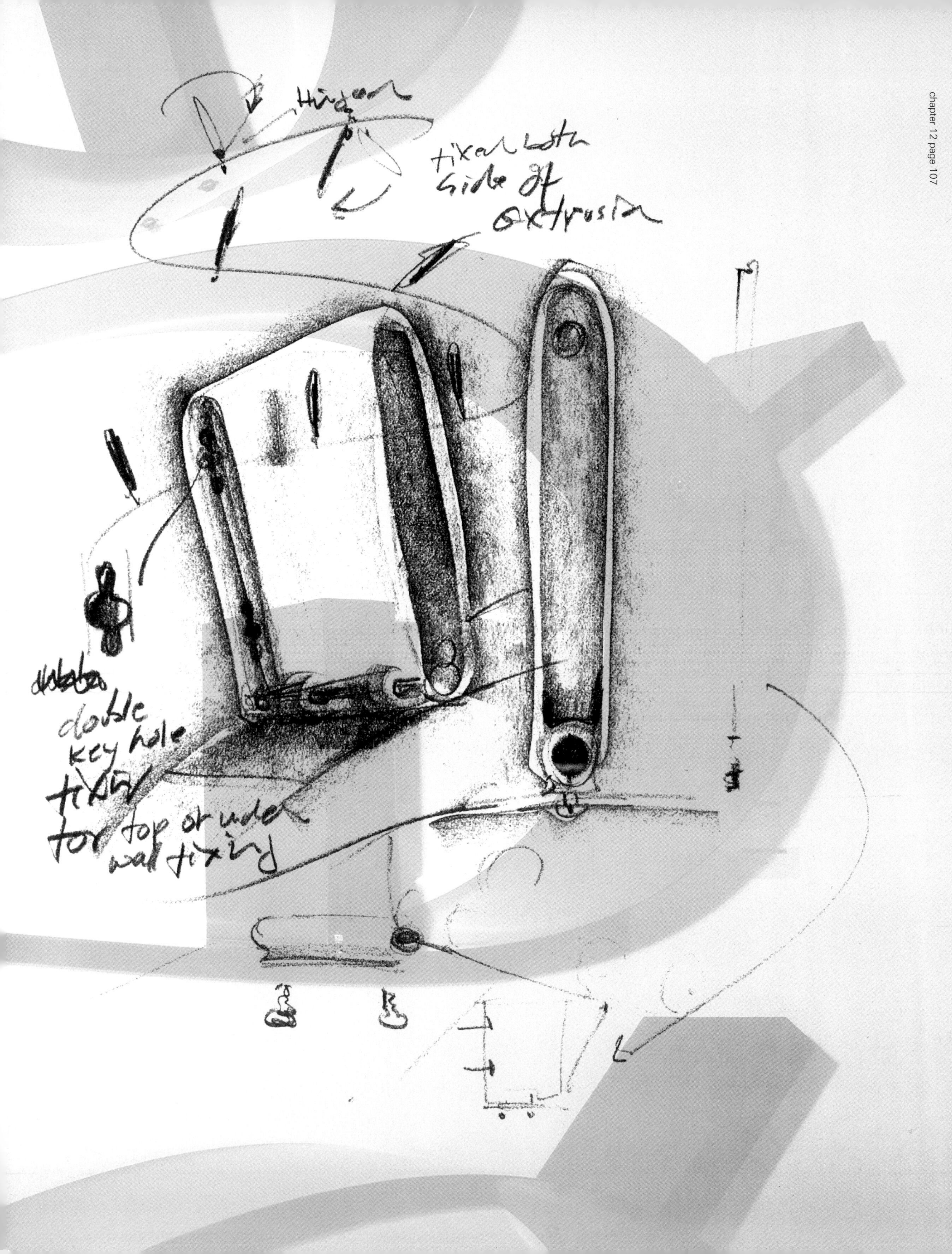
Hinged
fixed both side of extrusion
double key hole fixing
for top or under wall fixing

13

FOR YOUNG PEOPLE SETTING UP HOMES, LOW PRODUCTION COSTS IN THE FAR EAST, SELLING HIGH DESIGN TO THE MARKET-PLACE ETC., ETC.

It took the Ikea PS range to really shake the Milanese furniture establishment. Here was design all but indistinguishable from the most innovatory of contemporary work. And yet, with the benefit of production lines in Poland and Yugoslavia working to massive production runs, the Swedish giant could afford to offer prices at a fraction of the cost of the Italians and sell its wares not in glossy showrooms on the Via della Spiga, but in giant tin shopping sheds. For an industry that had previously relied on a distribution system that protected it from price-cutting, and which had always been able to count on premium prices, it was a challenge that could not be ignored. The Italians were running the risk of being beaten not just on price, but on ideas too.

The response varied from those companies which concentrated even more fixedly on the top end of the market, to those that started acquiring the language of the focus group, and the conventional wisdoms of the marketing men. Equipped with their formulas, these companies went looking for fresh design talent and produced briefs for products that, as they saw it, addressed the needs of a new generation of less affluent consumers, to whom they had to appeal if they were not to lose touch with reality. Arad found himself courted by companies as varied as Driade, Fiam and Guzzini, and producing furniture and objects that enjoyed mixed success.

For Fiam, a company that has long specialized in using high-profile designers to make signature products, Arad was a logical new name to add to the collection. And his glass storage system was an elegant product that sold well, even if it was untypical of his work. For Driade, despite its ambitions to address a younger generation, with low-cost products, the system remained expensive.

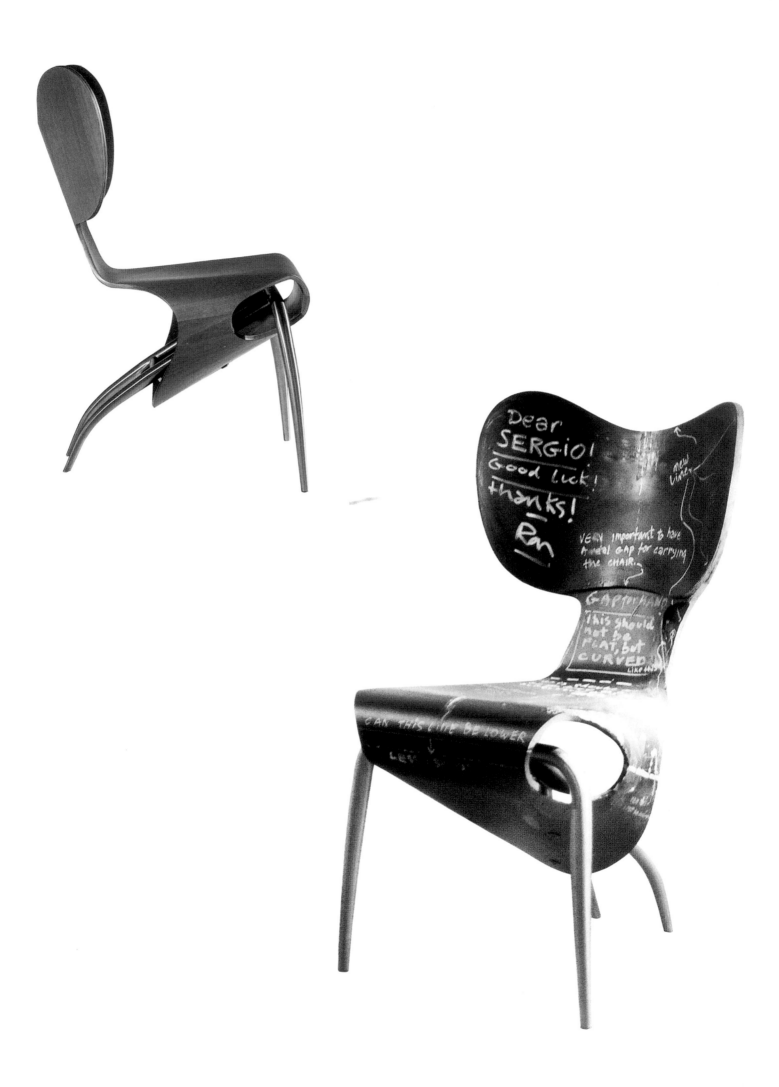

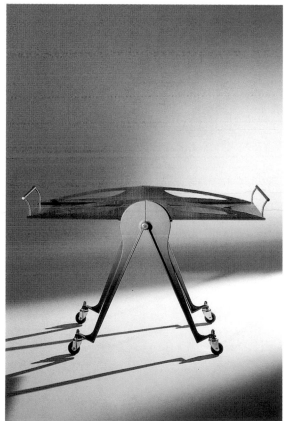

The Empty Chair, Driade, 1994 (opposite). This chair was initially designed for the Tel Aviv Opera House. Made of plywood and steel, it formed part of a range of pieces in ply for Driade which also included the folding tea trolley T44 (above) and the Fly Ply table (top right). The Fly Ply table has a double set of legs in cast aluminium at two different heights for dining or lounge use. The Zigo and Zago chairs, 1993, also for Driade (following pages) are stacking chairs with a steel rod structure made in one continuous hoop.

WE CAN BUT WAIT (OPTIMISTICALLY) AND SEE

The Fondation Cartier in Paris (completed in 1994) is anything but the conventional model of a building designed to accommodate the visual arts. It is transparent, indeterminate and open, rather than solid, rigidly defined and enclosed. Jean Nouvel, the architect, has designed a structure without a façade. Instead, the building comprises a series of glass layers, some outside the climatized perimeter, others contained within it. In one of those curious conjunctions of apparent opposites, the layered glass is simultaneously transparent and reflective. At night, when the artificial light comes on, the building seems entirely transparent, yet it is no longer possible to see through it, nor to find any reflections in its now invisible glass skin. These are the kind of paradoxes that have always appealed to Arad. And their creative exploitation is based on an understanding and a manipulation of the actual behaviour of materials. It is an understanding which has helped to shape the work of the studio in a variety of different forms over the years.

The Fondation Cartier offers no architectural alibis. There is no prospect of even the most vestigial of fig leaves of comfort for the kind of art that relies on the trappings of the gallery for its effect. There is no protection, and no shelter. Rather, its architecture is the very essence of transparency, and art within this framework is left mercilessly exposed, to sink or swim thanks only to its own intrinsic merits. There is an ambiguity about its spatial definition, about how the interior is contained, and about where its edges lie. Rather than being sharply defined, it appears to imply the possibility of infinite extension, of transience and transformation. Inside the gallery space there is an even more pressing ambiguity. The street on one side and the garden on the other are co-opted as part of the interior to become as much, if not

more, of a presence as a conventional wall, or a ceiling. Except of course that they are defined by elements that are not static but which constantly shift and redefine themselves.

This was the spatial context on offer when, as part of the programme of events which celebrated the establishment of the Fondation Cartier in its own purpose-designed building, Arad was invited to make a special installation for the entrance floor of Nouvel's building. And it offers an important insight into understanding the nature of his approach to design, his enthusiasms and the relationship of his work to that of other designers and architects.

Paris has given a sympathetic hearing to Arad ever since he was one of a group of designers invited by the Pompidou Centre to take part in an exhibition to mark its tenth anniversary (see page 49). Compared with work done earlier in Paris, Arad's answer to Nouvel's architecture was no less powerful, but altogether smoother and achieved with great economy of means. It was the product not just of the specific circumstances of the space itself, but also of a personal relationship with Nouvel.

For the Cartier, the raw material was nothing more elaborate than a series of tables that, structurally at least, were fairly straightforward. There were forty in all, each with a free-form, blade-thin, highly reflective steel top, mounted on the simplest of steel legs. They came in a variety of sizes, and with a range of shapes working around a central theme: nipped-in waists and rounded ends that flared outwards. They were indisputably at the right height at which to sit: there was nothing to get in the way of using them conventionally, by drawing up a chair to one and spreading out a newspaper to read, or laying a place for a meal. But put them together, in the context of Nouvel's building, and you got an alternative to the conventional idea of pragmatic furniture, even if the tables were light and portable enough to be easily accommodated in a couple of modestly sized trucks. In their shape and their materials, and especially in their essential ambiguity, they were clearly part of a personal language of design.

The table surfaces became part of a single, highly reflective group of objects, one that entirely changed the spatial quality of the gallery. They formed a pattern that reflected glass, sunlight, sky, trees and of course the people who tried to squeeze themselves in and around the gaps between the tables for a closer look during the period that they were being exhibited. The patterns

created between objects gave a sense of a double-take, of positive and negative existing side by side. The individual tables appeared to vanish; their mirror-like finish left them weightless and insubstantial. It was as if the ground floor of the gallery had been turned into a metal pond, or a pool filled to the lip with mercury. The dazzling puddles of smooth metal disrupted perceptions of the height of the space. Was the apparent depth, revealed in the reflections of the metal surface, genuinely the true distance down to the floor, or was the level of the table surface the true datum level? Or was it the all but invisible structural floor level 900 millimetres beneath?

The installation accentuated the blurring of exterior and interior, and finessed the dividing line between the two. The table tops reflected Nouvel's steel structure, at the same time as the raw metal finishes of the x-braced steel

The Fondation Cartier, Paris, 1994. Designed by Jean Nouvel, the Fondation Cartier is constructed from layers of glass. When illuminated at night, the building appears entirely transparent. Arad was invited to design the inaugral installation for the entrance floor. **The installation (opposite) was a series of forty mirror-polished stainless steel tables which offered transparency on the horizontal plane, complementing the reflective, transparent nature of the vertical planes.**

structure were echoed in the materials used for the tables. Inside and outside, reflection and reality, apparent and actual depth were permanently in tension, simultaneously deeper and shallower than they appeared, creating a perpetual oscillation that gave not just the work itself, but the space in which it is located, a resonating quality. The installation was a kind of perceptual yo-yo, that had one's pupils constantly refocusing to cope with the surfeit of data with which one was continually bombarded. The installation was to be read on two levels: as pragmatic product design, or as a more culturally ambitious work.

A similar piece exists in London's Belgo Noord restaurant, where the table's practical meaning comes first. Although in the restaurant the formal perfection of the newly completed installation rapidly gives way to the

dulling impact of the constant abrasions of everyday use, the two categories of object start out looking almost identical. Solid, polished metal reflects itself, the room around it, the drinks placed on its surface, and the faces of those on either side of the counter. Here, the tables are not objects that invite contemplation, but are functional artefacts on which to eat moules and frites rather than a means of mediating a space.

In Paris, the installation was just as much a powerful spatial disrupter as Nouvel's architecture. It was executed with a clear appreciation of not only Jeff Koons' metal casts of inflatable plastic rabbits, but also of the reflective surfaces of Richard Wilson's bath of sump oil and steel, originally made in 1987 and now installed at the Saatchi Gallery in London. Wilson's work is powerful for its use of the reflective quality of stagnant oil to create a

An early sketch for the Fondation Cartier installation (below). The sequential mirroring effect of the tables created a waist-high floating surface (left). The '38 Tables' installation at the Milan Triennale in 1995 (poster opposite) was a variation on the Fondation Cartier exhibition.

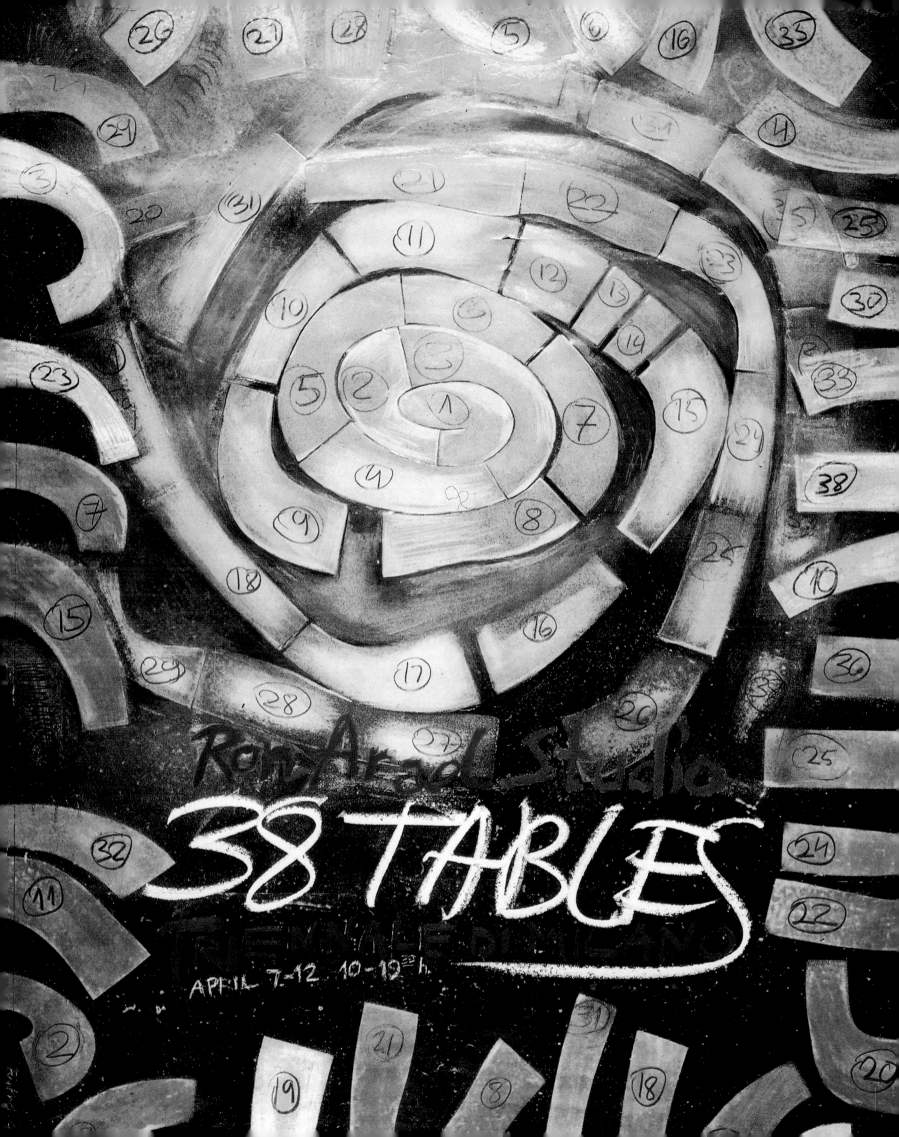

dizzying sense of weightlessness, and the way it disrupts the space in which it is located. It was a precedent of which Arad was well aware.

For any designer, the reflective surface is interesting in the way that it explores the fundamental idea of space. It plays with visual and tactile perceptions to distort and camouflage, and to manipulate perceptions and expectations, and denies the evidence supplied by the senses. It plays tricks with perception. It allows design to escape from the constraints of a single-minded approach to form, and offers the possibility of an object with a chameleon-like existence, borrowing the attributes of its surroundings. The results, sometimes controlled, sometimes random and accidental, have the

effect of rippling the surface of the larger pieces of furniture. At the same time that they make considerable play with formal values, they give heavy objects the effect of buoyancy.

And in a period in which the seductive tyranny of the charismatic object seems to have outrun its course, the quality of reflection is a possible way out of the dilemma for the designer who looks for a more allusive, elusive quality in design than simply the creation of more possessions, to trap our definitions of each other and ourselves in questions of brand loyalty and taste and the usual signals of design manipulated to suggest the messages of consumerism.

'38 Tables', Milan Triennale, 1995 (opposite). Unlike the tables for the Cartier exhibition, the Triennale tables were from the start designed to be sold. These were real tables and so the detail was much more important (above). The structure could accommodate table tops of any shape or size. The tables recall Jean Prouvé's Compass table. The lights for the Triennale installation were designed by Ingo Maurer.

Belgo Noord, London, 1994. The
Cartier table was later developed
and used in this restaurant. It had
become a real table around which
one large group of people or two
separate groups could sit.

Chair by its Cover, Why Bark?, Why Dog? and Reflection on Another Chair, 1989–90. These pairs of found chairs are each embraced by a 'volume' envelope with a highly reflective inner surface. On the back of one chair there is an inscription in mirrored letters which reads 'Why bark when you have a dog' and on the other 'Why have a dog if you can bark'.

15

FREEZE-DRIED MICE NEXT TO PUFFING BILLY

Is it Ron Arad's work that we are looking at, or is it the first genetically engineered mouse, preserved after it had given its life for science by refrigeration that draws our attention? The museum curator and the exhibition organizer have become increasingly interested in the ability of the designer to create a context for their work. As audiences have become jaded, it is the designer's task to create the sense of occasion and performance that can draw people away from their televisions, and impress even those who have become sated with the imagery of the department store and the advertising video. The techniques vary: at the Science Museum, design would have been pushed to the background. At Louisiana, where the objective was a temporary exhibition of British design, Arad's work was very much in the foreground. But the objective is the same; to present objects as a cultural phenomenon, rather than as a mere spectacle.

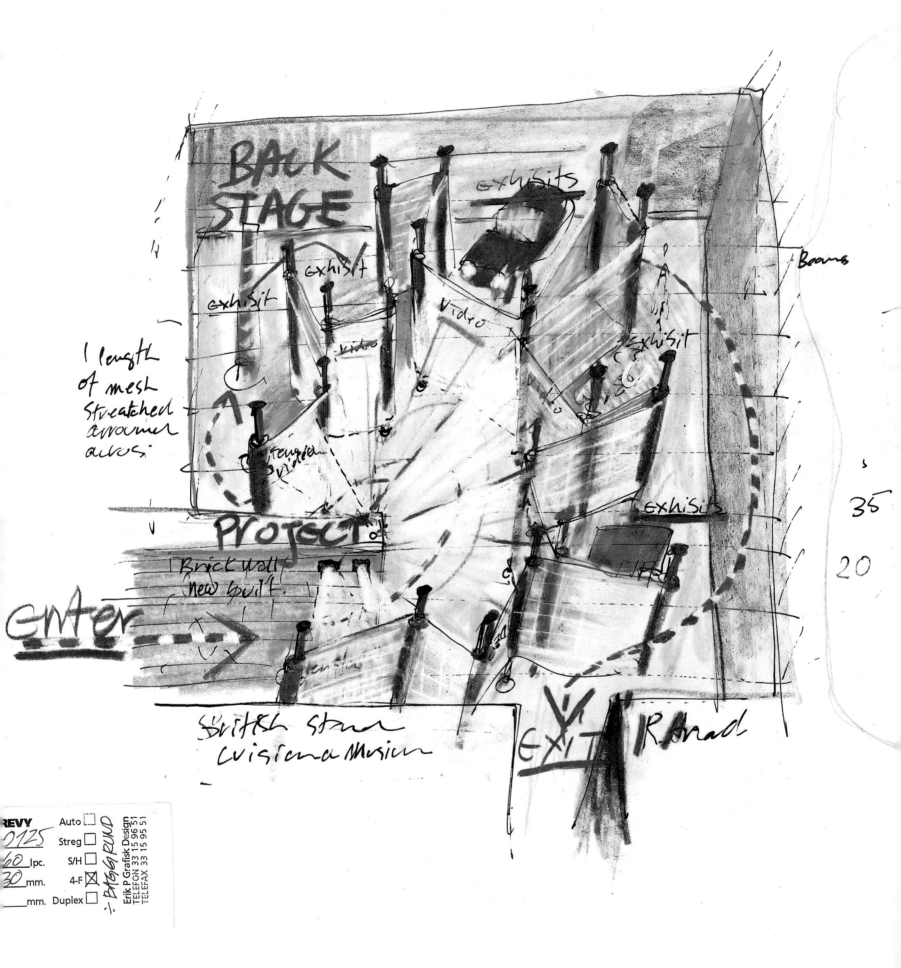

BACK STAGE

exhibits

exhibit

exhisit

Video

exhibit

1 length of mesh streatched arround across.

Video

exhibits

PROJECT

Brick wall new built.

ENTER

British Stand Luisiana Museum

EXIT R.Arad

Booms

35

20

Louisiana Museum of Modern Art,
Denmark, 1996. Concept and
layout design for the British Room
in the 'Design and Identity' exhibition. One section of the exhibition
focused on British advertising
with a video projecting on to a
stainless steel tensioned mesh
enclosure, another on original
British products that represented
innovative technical solutions.

'Making of the Modern World', 1997. A competition entry for the design of the Science Museum gallery, London, accommodating the route to the new Welcome Wing. As well as providing easy access to the new wing, the gallery had to display icon exhibits. In RAA's entry a 'flyover' crossed the space, giving views of the exhibits on slow turntables to the left and right of it. Smaller, secondary displays were accommodated under the flyover. The balustrade provided digital information on the exhibits, allowing them to remain uncluttered by text or signage.

16

SPORT

In the early 1990s, the dividing line between sportswear and fashion evaporated: certain people started getting nostalgic about the earliest generation of off-the-track trainers. The first time around, it was a question of appropriating the muscular glamour of the athletics stadium with a straight face. Thus the entirely sedentary could bask in the reflected glory of the super-fit simply by wearing to the supermarket supposedly specialized equipment crafted for high performance. The second coming of the trainer was marked by knowingness layered on knowingness. They were designed to appeal to the young and fashionable: those without the faintest interest in javelin throwing or relay racing, who could date a shoe's original appearance to the nearest month from the minutest fluctuations in stitching and colour. The imagery of sport became an essential part of the fashion designer's repertoire, and as a result, sportswear lost its innocence. It was styled to look fashionable. And while it was important to continue to trade on the idea of authentic sport, the big sportswear brands needed to respond to a wider context as well. The swooshes and stripes came to dominate the landscape of the club and the street as well as the arena. Given that context, Nike and Adidas had no choice but to start behaving in the way that a fashion house would, carefully fostering the power of their brand, but at the same time extending it as far as it could go in their endless struggle for credibility and visibility. Which is why in the mid 1990s Adidas planned to build a flagship store for its products on the Champs Elysées in Paris, not a location commonly associated with sport. And that is why it took so much trouble about its design, inviting Arad to compete with no less than Alfredo Arribas and Jean Nouvel for the commission.

The winning design was never built, a decision that came when the family-run business appointed a new managerial team. But it did lead to a series of Adidas Sports Cafés, an attempt by a French brewery to exploit the lure of the Adidas identity. And it was a significant departure for Arad, both for its intrinsic quality, and for its working method. The store, carved from a stone-fronted classical building once used as a cinema, was a complex piece of

architectural design and spatial planning. It displayed a striking series of technical innovations based on physical and electronic illusions, and it also involved, for the first time, extensive use of computer modelling techniques. Where metal cutters and welders in the workshop previously had given Arad the space to perfect his designs, computers took on the same role for the Adidas shop.

'When I first saw the project and the building that Adidas were on the verge of buying, I thought, "Oh good, it's a roof project." It had previously been a cinema, with a kind of innocent façade, a little dilapidated. And I thought right away that it was going to be all about leaving the front alone, and putting the muscle into doing an amazing whatever on the roof. But it didn't turn out to be that at all. Adidas wanted to call it The Stadium, and I was bugged by the name. I thought it sounded a bit cheap. What stadium? Where is it? And that triggered off the idea of a *trompe l'oeil* stadium. I would never make something that is there just for decoration. It wasn't going to be just a fake stadium, but the underbelly of the stadium, placed right at the front of the building, seemed like a very strong idea for an entrance.'

While retaining the bulk of the original 19th-century façade, Arad would have treated visitors to a series of spectacles. The entrance would have sucked people in under a projecting curved overhang, its stepped profile a convincing re-creation of the haunches of a raked stadium stand. The space was wide enough for no more than a narrow pie-shaped slice, but Arad wedged it between mirror walls that would have had the effect of completing the illusion. Movement through the store would have taken a dramatic zigzag course, tacking back and forth through the various departments, providing a scene worthy of a flagship store for the Adidas brand. Indeed, this wasn't meant to be a place to go to merely to complete the mundane transaction of buying a football shirt or a pair of running shoes. It was envisaged as somewhere special that created the sense of a shared spectacle, of being as much an event as a shop.

The multi-screen video wall has become a commonplace in sportswear retailing, and the Adidas commission would have taken this much further. Arad was looking at ways in which the running feet of athletes could be projected on to the side of escalator walls to match the customers' bodies.

'It was a one-way travelator that gave you a pair of sporty legs at random. You could have walked in on Steffi Graff's legs. Then the escalator would spit you out into the store, after you had been sucked in. The problem was how to follow a strong entrance, how to avoid an anti-climax. I never looked at the plan and designed from it. I started in the entrance and moved on from there. It was like choreography, doing it piece by piece, until each one gelled, and then we moved on. We thought that it would have the world's biggest realtime scoreboard, full of mixed sources of media, from old-fashioned telex to fax and pixel. Even the lift became interactive.'

The Adidas competition came at a moment at which Arad's working methods and objectives were in a state of flux. With the agreement with the Italian metal fabricator, Ronchetti, to take on responsibility for the fabrication of One Off products, and the old workshop dismantled, the studio shifted direction quickly. It filled up with architects rather than makers. And in the One Off workshop, which had once struggled with sheet metal, larger and larger computer monitors and more and more architectural model-makers appeared where there had once been oxyacetylene cylinders.

'When we packed up the workshop to transfer production to Italy, we found a space where the workshop used to be. We thought about what we would ideally want there for the office's future, and we came up with computer imaging and model-making. I said to Oliver Salway, who was studying architecture at the Bartlett, and was as interested in new media as in architecture, "Why don't you set up here?" I didn't really know what he was going to do and Adidas was the first project that we did together. When we interviewed Berni Keenan for her job as an assistant, she mentioned that her boyfriend was in the Arup model-making team, and was looking to set up on his own. So they both came, and there it was: we could design upstairs and work with both the computers and model-makers downstairs. It was a competition between the real model and the computer image, but the similarity was very exciting, the virtual and the real, which in turn was almost simultaneous with it being designed. It is a machine that you have to feed, we were always late to provide information. Never before have clients really known what they are about to get, because nobody can really read architectural drawings. And here, you sit them in front of the screen, and they see exactly what they are going to get. That relationship affects the work, both for

Preliminary sketches for the Adidas Stadium competition, 1996.

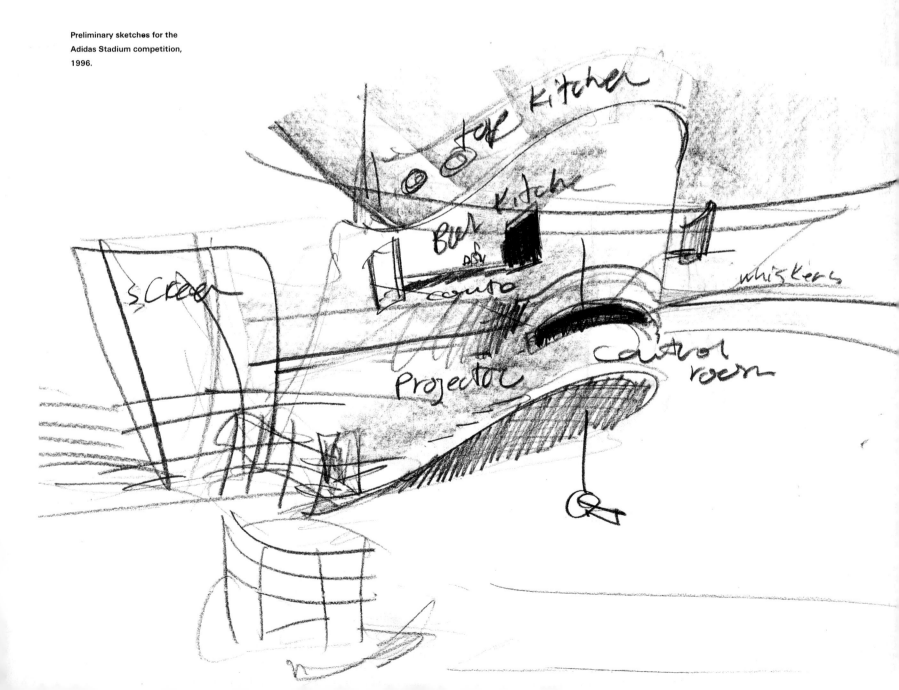

the client and for the designer, because you get used to things. You see it very fast. Maybe there is some sort of imprinting: it becomes harder to change because we know it so well, and it would be hard to do. A lot of work you see now is computer generated. You can see it in new cars: they use this program or that program. My drawing has declined, but there is still a demand for a

hairy, handmade sketch. Once it was easy, now it needs thinking about.'

The issue was not simply a technical one.

'Designing with the computer is not so much like getting a photograph of what you have in mind before it's made: it's like seeing it in a film. It's like

knowing the sex of your child in advance. We have renderings now that look more real than photographs. You have to make sure what you do gets more "wow" when it is actually made.'

Computer images of the Adidas Stadium interior and façade. Travelator ramps criss-cross the main volume of the space in a figure of eight (right). The giant interactive wall contains a variety of media transmitting the latest sports results, live satellite coverage and LCD bulletin boards. The video installation on the façade shows black and white footage of Adidas heroes (below right).

Trompe l'oeil entrance to the Champs Elysées building (above). The mirror-edged wedge creates an illusion of the underbelly of a stadium. The side panels of the travelator provide each person entering with a pair of 'virtual legs' during their journey across to the main space. In the Sports Café on the top floor of the Adidas Stadium (below left), adjustable LCD screens hover over tables.

The Adidas Sport Café, Toulon, 1997. Carbon fibre tubes are flattened every 1.8 metres (5.9 feet) to accommodate two LCD screens back to back at each set of cantilevered tables. The Kartell FPE chair was developed for the Adidas Sport Cafés.

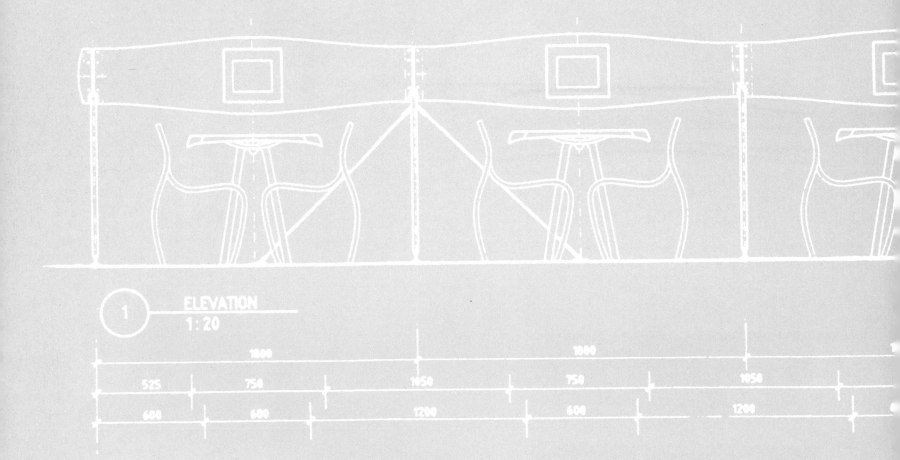

① ELEVATION 1:20

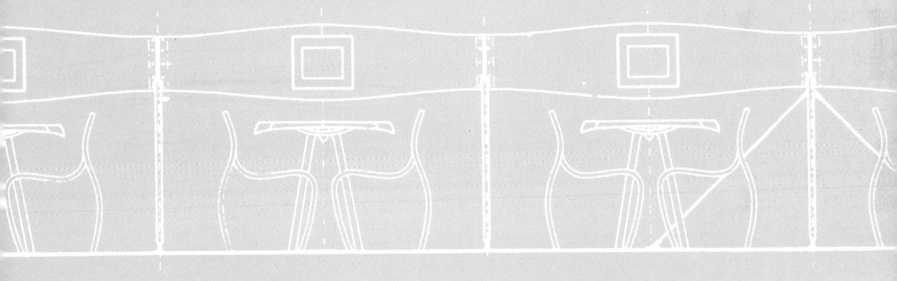

FANTASTIC PLASTIC ELASTIC

The FPE is not a chair that depends on a signature, nor which relies for its impact on a designer's single attention-grabbing gesture. Nor is it a design that is overwhelmed by the desire to make a big show of being formally inventive simply for the sake of being original. It is about Arad accepting the game of design on its own terms rather than side-stepping to come up with an oblique response. It is about making a chair on an industrial scale, and as a result, attempting to simplify the problems of manufacture by taking things away, rather than by adding non-essentials.

The piece has its origins in a commission to design an exhibition stand for Mercedes, to be used at motor shows around Europe. The idea was to demonstrate Mercedes' attention to detail by going to the lengths of producing a chair specifically for the stand. But given the cost penalties that come from trying to make a chair without the benefit of economies of scale, it had to be made as cheaply as possible: with no scope to amortize tooling costs on a long production run, it had to avoid elaborate manufacturing techniques. This almost inevitably meant a wooden seat and back, while a primitive sand-cast aluminium structure was the only alternative to bent tubular steel. The appropriate mass-production approach – given a sufficiently generous budget – would have been a pressure-cast structure which didn't make economic sense for the number of chairs involved. But the chair

did have a quiet simplicity and a formal logic and Arad looked to see if it could be made into a practical reality by resurrecting it for a number of subsequent projects.

At the time of the competition to design the Adidas store in Paris, the idea of a specially designed chair surfaced again: this time in an extruded plastic rather than cast metal. Kartell, with whom Arad explored the idea, said that it was still too expensive for the likely number of chairs involved – 'Please think of something else'. That led to a further simplification: a double-barrelled structure based on two tubes, cut staggered, leaving one short, and one long tube, with absolutely no waste. The extrusion is bent to form the profile of the chair. The seat and back are made from a plastic membrane, which remains flexible until you sit on the chair, when the weight of the occupant locks the structure and makes it rigid. In its production version, the chair uses an injection-moulding, but a very cheap one. The bulk of a production tool is what makes it expensive, but the tubes required in this chair are almost flat, which in turn means almost no material, and a minimal bulk for the tool. Applying the seat membrane is an equally ingenious process. It is only when the tubing is bent that the profile closes, which has the effect of locking the seat in place, without any rivets.

The Cross Your T's chair, 1996
(opposite below). This chair, a
cast aluminium T-section with a
bent ply seat, was designed for
Mercedes Benz's own use and
produced by hand in small
quantities. The design was not
considered suitable for mass-
production and led Arad to devel-
op the more refined, industrially
made Fantastic Plastic Elastic
chair (above and opposite top).

The Fantastic Plastic Elastic
(FPE) chair, Kartell, 1997. The
transparent plastic seat is
inserted into double-barrelled
aluminium extrusions prior to
bending. The process of bending
the chair to shape causes the
extrusion to 'bite' the plastic,
thereby fixing together the parts
without glue or screws.

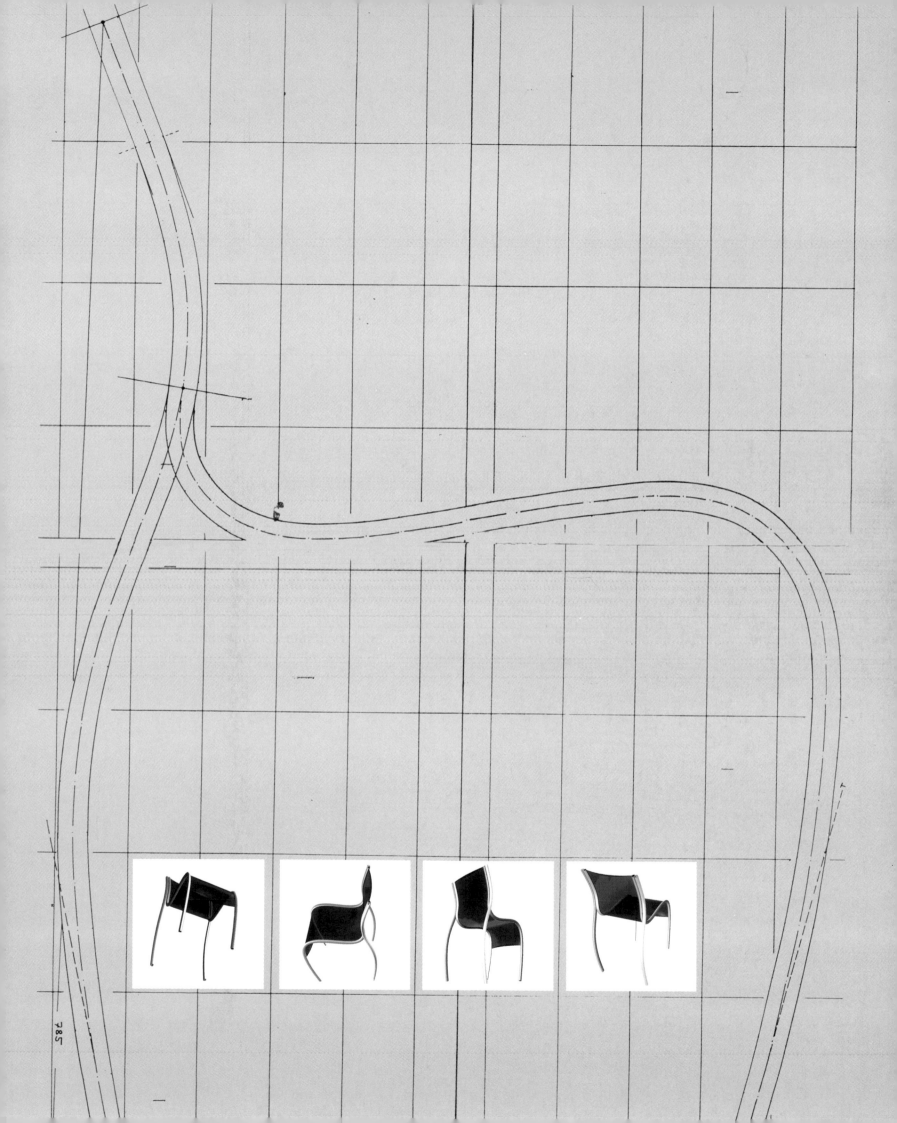

THE READY-TO-WEAR RTW

The idea of the object that never sits still is a recurring dream. The table that turns into a wall-hanging, the steel mat that turns into an armchair, and here, the storage unit that takes the form of a wheel. Push it around a room with fingertip pressure and the ball-bearings in its inner rim keep the storage surfaces horizontal. Like the Bookworm, it started in steel, and thanks to Kartell, turned into something else.

The RTW, 1996 (left). A series of free-spinning wheels of storage. The aluminium shelves locked within the inner wheel always remain level with the floor, while the outer wheel can be rolled at will. Translucent radially sliding doors 'digitize' the light penetrating from behind. Computer visuals of modifications to prepare the RTW for industrial production in plastic (opposite).

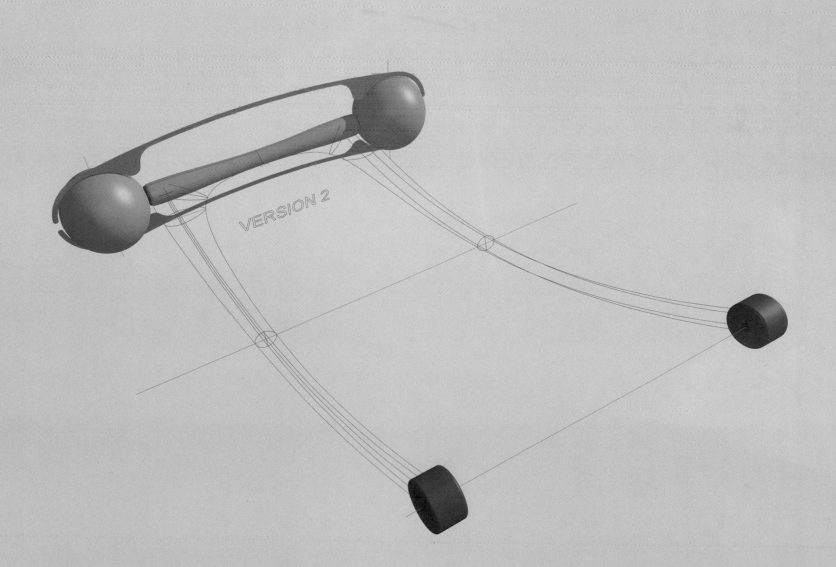

VERSION 2

MAYBE A HYPER-REALISTIC SCULPTURE OF ONE HUNDRED STACKING CHAIRS

Design is often a matter of putting together familiar elements in unfamiliar ways, of transferring ideas that originate in one setting to completely different contexts, and in the process discovering in them entirely new possibilities. Something very like that underlied the sequence of chairs which emerged from a commission from the critic and newly appointed editor of *Domus*, François Burckhardt. This involved the creation of a landmark in the centre of Milan to promote the magazine during the 1997 Furniture Fair. *Domus* needed to make a splash: Burckhardt talked about creating a hyper-realistic sculpture of a hundred stacking chairs. It was the starting point not just for a genuine temporary landmark (even if it wasn't quite a hundred chairs high), but for two versions of a limited-edition chair in different materials, which then mutated into the preliminaries for a mass-produced chair.

The aesthetic origins of the project derive from a commission to design a dining room in a house outside Tel Aviv. A dining table of adjustable length was part of the brief and it seemed like an interesting idea to consider it in terms of linking a varying number of circular elements, two or more of which could be used to make up a table of appropriate length. The units would be dropped into place in a detachable ring, a little like the plastic rings used to hold six-packs of beer cans together. When not in use, the rings could hang on the wall. The sketches for the table showed a profile distinguished by a series of ridges. At the time, a chair to match the table was also a possibility, and it seemed important to use a profile that echoed those ridged lines. This was the chair that came into Arad's mind when he had his conversation with Burckhardt about the *Domus* project.

A freehand sketch emerged that showed the essence of the chair, with the seat and back made from a single element, moulded with a circular rippling profile. The tower would be made by stacking enough chairs to make an impact on Milan's streetscape. Just as critical for the genesis of the project was the technical issue. As time was very short for the piece to be ready for the Fair, the chairs would have to be capable of being manufactured quickly and economically. At one time, the drawing would have been taken into the workshop in order for a model-maker to realize it in three-dimensions. Now, the studio could manipulate it in Photoshop. The process gave the idea of a single chair from every conceivable angle, as well as a rendering that showed it as a stacking chair. The shortcoming of this procedure, of course,

was that it appeared to stack, but without a lot of design work, it would remain an anomalous phantom image, an Escher diagram. The image did not reflect a physical reality. The drawing and the computer image formed the basis for a full-size glass-fibre model. It provided some intrinsic clues for manufacturing. The back was clearly going to be shorter than the seat, so it seemed to make sense, if it was going to be moulded out of a single piece of material, to make the ripples deeper and shorter in the back, and to have them more spaced out, and shallower, in the seat.

At that stage, even the material was in doubt. The studio, after giving over its one-offs to Ronchetti, had no manufacturing capacity of its own.

'I didn't know how to make the chair in plastic. It would have been possible, but it would have taken two moulds, which would have been too expensive.'

The way forward came from the technical expertise of a specialist manufacturer, Superform Aluminium, responsible, among much else, for the cladding of Norman Foster's Sainsbury Centre, but with no experience in Arad's area of design. The company, which specializes in precision-engineered aluminium components, had never worked on furniture before, but it saw no reason to believe it wasn't up to the relatively straightforward task of making a chair in aluminium. It offered the chance to make tooling at a relatively low cost which could, if not exactly mass-produce a chair, then at least make it rapidly in reasonable quantities. Superform took the studio-made fibreglass model away to its factory in Worcester to analyse its shape. The company's technicians were back in less than a week, this time bringing their own computer in the boot of their Mondeo. It came with the Katia program, developed by Marcel Dassault's aerospace technicians to analyse complex wing-surface forms, and with it Superform were able to demonstrate the exact profile that the chair would need to adopt to be capable of being manufactured in formed aluminium. The computer design work was relatively quick. To make the tool that would actually be used to press aluminium into a one-piece chair took longer. It began with a lump of steel weighing three tons. Superform Aluminium have a computerized tool-making program which turns the computer image of the tool into physical reality. Something like a domestic carving knife was programmed to spend two weeks peeling away at the steel to make an extraordinarily intricate tool. Not only did it produce

the exact profile needed, but because the aluminium is vacuum-formed, the tool needed a network of minute air-holes like underground canals, cut with a tiny 10mm drill. The process was so delicate that at least one of the drills broke inside the half-formed mould, and work had to start again.

In unit terms, the chair is probably the cheapest piece of furniture to emerge from the Arad studio to date, although it did take twenty minutes between product cycles to use the tool to make another chair (as it would heat up and then be allowed to cool down). This was not exactly mass-production as would have been recognized in a conventional furniture factory, but it did allow the project to be completed in just three months.

Vitra were involved with the project from the early stages (their own version, retailing at high street prices and requiring the massive investment needed to make the tooling for an injection-moulded version in plastic, was launched at the Cologne Furniture Fair in 1998 – see page 194). But Arad also had

the problem of dealing with his own Milan Fair exhibition, for the first time without a workshop of his own. He took the basic form of the chair and made a simplified version in fibreglass. Apart from having no ripples, it had the same form that could become the basis for a limited edition. Paradoxically, this resulted in the most expensive version of the chair, reflecting the countless hours that Arad had to spend in Millennium Model's tiny workshop in the studio basement working on the chairs himself, and there is a touch of the bucket and spade about it. It was this fact that in part accounts for the decorated version.

'You can't sell a dining chair for £5,000 unless it has some art in it. To paint a decorative chair can easily fall on the wrong side of kitsch. When you work almost in public, you have to carry on regardless. It was messy stream of consciousness. It could have flopped but it worked, though it is always a tight-rope. Some of the individual chairs are sort of ugly ducklings, but once they are in a group they start to work.'

Tom Vac, 1997. A superplastic aluminium vacuum-formed shell ribbed with gradually flattening concentric circles and mounted on a stainless steel frame, the Tom Vac chair was designed and produced in only four months.

The development of the chair was speeded up to meet the deadline for the Totem, a landmark made up of 100 stacking chairs commissioned by *Domus* magazine for the centre of Milan.

The Tom Vac chair, 1997: detail
and stacked.

Carbo Tom, 1997. A carbon fibre
version of Tom Vac. A vacuum-
formed aluminium shell was
used as the mould for this limited
edition chair.

Pic Chairs, 1997. Twenty handmade fibreglass, resin and pigment chairs loosely based on the shape of Tom Vac (here and previous pages). Each chair is unique and includes a variety of media – tissues, newspaper, pure pigments and luminous wire. The group is in the collection of the Mourmans Gallery.

Uncut, 1997. A vacuum-formed
aluminium chair on a low
stainless steel structure, Uncut
is an untrimmed version of Tom
Vac. The chair exists in mirror-
polished aluminium (opposite)
and anodized aluminium (above).

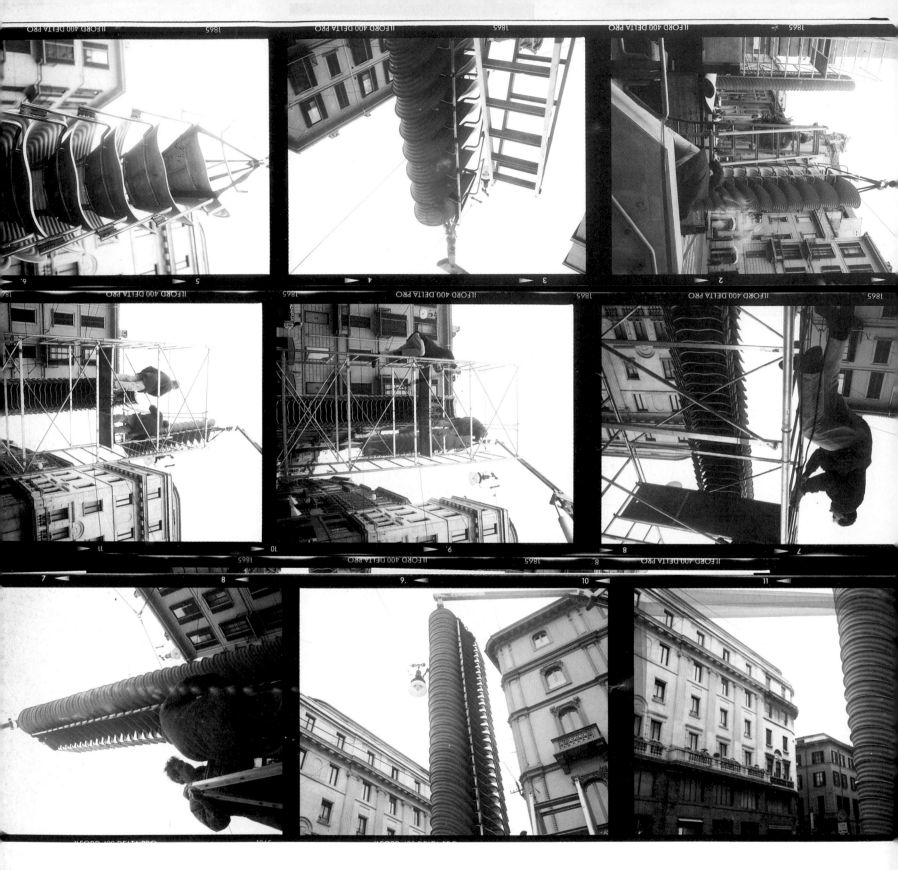

Constructing the *Domus* Totem in
the centre of Milan.

The *Domus* Totem, Milan, 1997. The Totem consisted of 10 metres (33 feet) of stacking Tom Vac chairs. The gaps between the chairs became gradually wider towards the top. The lighting was hidden in the spaces between the chairs. The top chair was a pixel board displaying information controlled from a remote computer.

IT DOESN'T EVEN HAVE A PROPER ROOF

Shortly after Tony Blair came to power in May 1997, New Labour staged a party in Downing Street to parade its commitment to design as one of Britain's vital new creative industries. It was a remarkable event, which saw the culture minister, Chris Smith, minister for the Dome, Peter Mandelson, as well as Blair himself in the same room as John Pawson, Ross Lovegrove and Ron Arad among many others. For one evening at least, the neo-classical surroundings of Downing Street were co-opted by the young-guns of design.

This was a chance for a new administration to demonstrate that it took Britain's most innovative designers seriously: that it valued them as both a cultural and a financial force, capable of demonstrating that Britain was making a mark on the world creatively, and who could also provide it with an economic underpinning. New Labour might have embraced the idea of design as a positive force in the abstract, but they had not yet demonstrated that they had explored the intellectual consequences. This was exactly the moment at which Arad was working on an architectural project which put him in a position to question the depth of the new government's commitment – and the limitations of its ability to influence events.

At this time, Arad had recently been commissioned to take on a project that cut across the conventional wisdoms of the planning system built up over the previous two decades. New, it was assumed throughout the 1970s and 1980s, meant worse. And if you were going to build new, the sensitive approach was to model the new on what had gone before. Arad, on the other hand, was commissioned to design a new house in Hampstead, one of London's most culturally ambiguous environments. The commission involved tearing down an existing house, and the clients had chosen Arad expressly because he would not be prepared to mimic what had gone before.

The site was one of a series of quiet residential streets, originally laid out in the 1920s, that fringe Hampstead Heath. In those days it had been a marginal area, far removed from the cultural centre of the city. Over the years it had turned into a favoured enclave for the affluent. The street had originally been laid out as a sequence of detached houses, built by speculative developers in a debased form of the Arts and Crafts style that had, at the turn of the century, represented the most progressive manner available for builders. As time went on, the area attracted more prosperous people, who looked to expand the original homes, in part to meet their growing needs. But there was also the urge to make their mark – to take a modest cottage and enlarge it, simply as an exercise in its own right. It is a process that can be found in the most affluent suburbs of many cities, in Los Angeles and Paris as well as London. And it was an ongoing and cumulative process, repeated over several generations, adding layer upon layer to what were once relatively modest houses.

By the time that Arad came on the scene, what had originally been a cottage had been expanded on several occasions. The innate qualities the building once had were long since lost, and all the neighbouring houses had gone through the same process. Hence the wish to cut across the prevailing conventional wisdom. Rather than tinker with the house that already existed, Arad's clients were ready to start again, to tear down the property that they had acquired, and to ask Arad to design a house from scratch.

At any point in the 1980s, this would have seemed an impossible request. Britain in the era of the Prince of Wales's architectural debate was a country which automatically assumed that new meant worse than that which had gone before. Arad's clients did not subscribe to such a timid view of the world. And Arad was ready to go along with his clients' cultural assumptions: to put his neck on the line and come up with a design that started again. In the place of what had been a cosy Arts and Crafts vernacular design, albeit one that had been torn apart by three generations of later owners, he proposed an uncompromisingly fresh design: two interlocking egg-shaped shells. They had nothing to do with the language of affluent contemporary housing in North London. Nor did they have anything in common with the insipid language of brick and pitched tile roofs that had taken its place for

Amiga House, London, 1997–8.
A montage showing the house as
seen from the street (above). Site
plan and aerial view of the model
(opposite).

want of anything more rigorous. They were designed to be made using a composite carbon-fibre material, derived from boat-building techniques.

All this happened during an interlude in which such a bold move might have had, for the first time in two decades, at least a modest chance of success – as the gathering in Downing Street had demonstrated, the cultural assumptions of Britain were going through nothing less than a sea change.

Arad entered as a somewhat embattled figure. The design that he had put forward had not been well received – at least by some of the neighbouring householders, in particular the architect John Seifert who lived across the road and occupied a lumpish Dallas-style brick mansion. The scene was accordingly set for a battle between the vested interests of the status quo, and an attempt to build something fresh and new. In the previous two

decades, when Britain had taken fright at the prospect of anything that smacked of the new, there would not have been the remotest prospect of Arad's design having any chance of success. In a climate in which Arad was being invited to Downing Street as a representative of Britain's brightest and best talents, things had clearly changed. This was no longer a question which could automatically be met with a refusal by the local planning authority. Indeed, Arad found himself acquiring such unlikely allies as English Heritage, a body which would once have automatically defended the status quo, but which now chose to support Arad and his design as offering the best chance of producing a new building that would look towards the future. Arad was able, at that Downing Street event, to enlist the support of a new generation of politicians for his project in a way that would have been unthinkable just a couple of years earlier. As things turned out, Haringey Council, the planning authority, was still moved to reject his application.

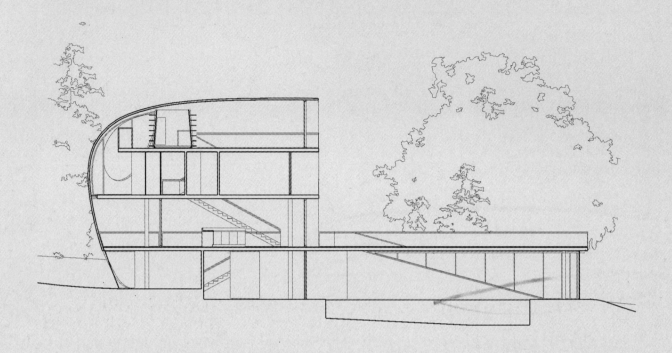

Amiga House model and
section view from the street
(opposite). The shells provide
privacy while also allowing a
view through to the garden.
View from the garden showing the spaces locked
between the rectangular
concrete structure and the
free-form shell (above). The
uninterrupted slab at ground
level allows a double-height
space under the lower shell
and extends as a terrace,
partially covering the swim-
ming pool. The taller shell
contains the dining area, and
a 'box' of two bedrooms with
the main bedroom above it.

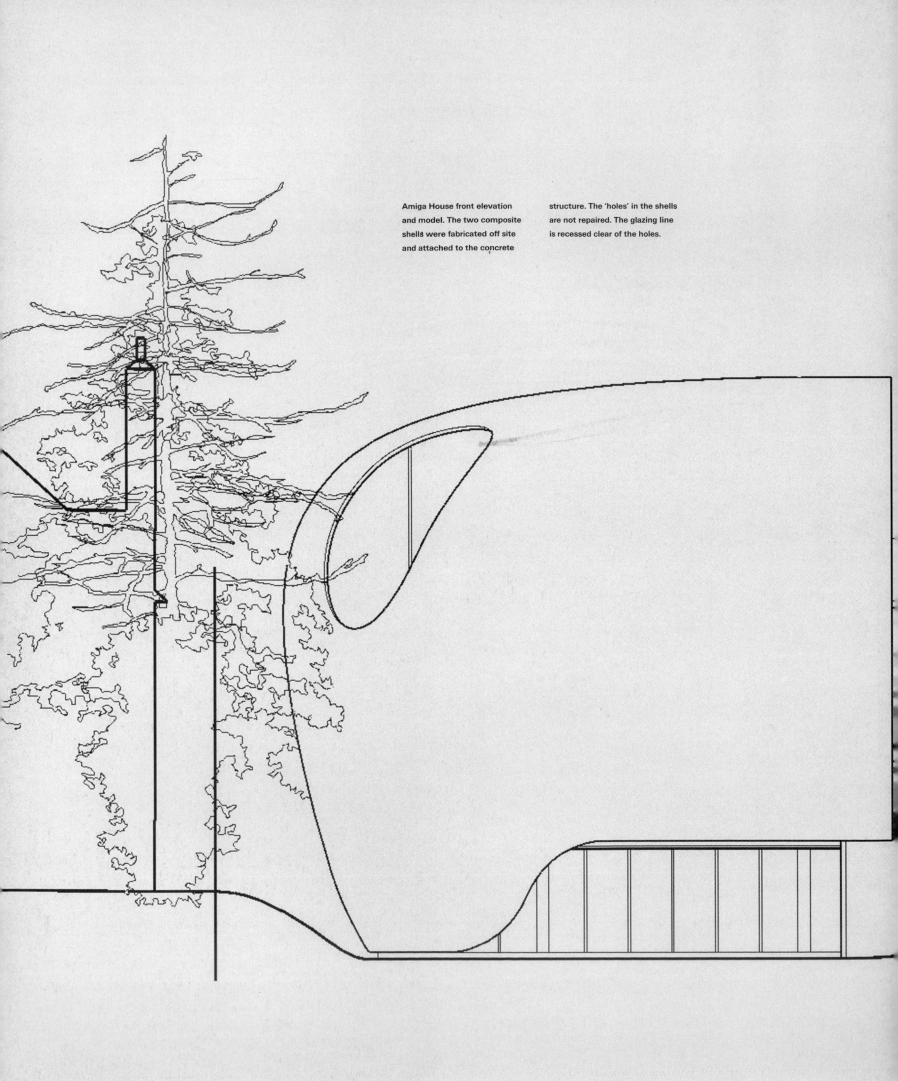

Amiga House front elevation and model. The two composite shells were fabricated off site and attached to the concrete structure. The 'holes' in the shells are not repaired. The glazing line is recessed clear of the holes.

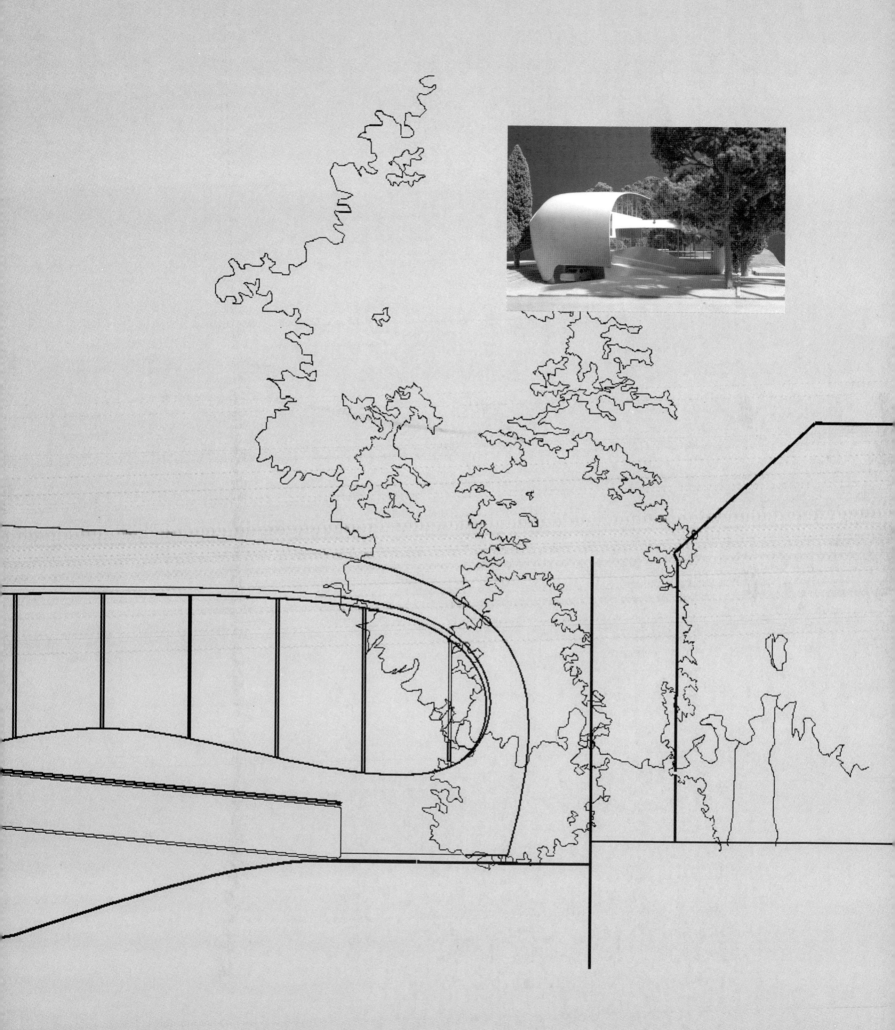

+419.9m

+416.7m

PROPOSED STUDIO

+419.9m

▽EL +418.51m

+416.7m

PROPOSED STUDIO   EXISTING HOUSE

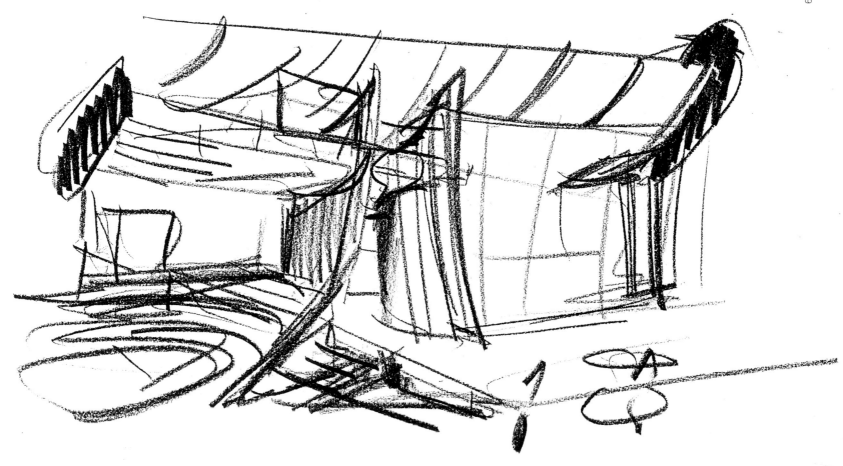

Private House/Publishing Studio,
Germany, 1993. Unbuilt proposal
for a hillside building in the Black
Forest. Twin conical timber roofs
of composite construction form
11-metre (36-foot) cantilevers
from two supporting cores,
dividing the building into a
double-height studio and a
private living area.

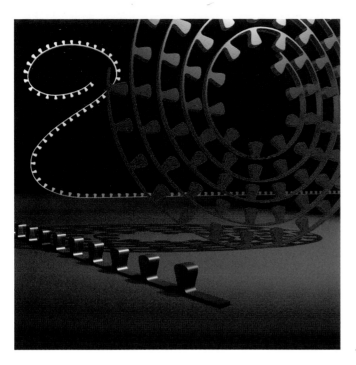

CALL IT RED TAPE

There was a time when Arad's exploration of the potential of creative scavenging was a survival strategy. It was a way of finding ready-processed materials that could give his work some of the attributes of high-tech manufacturing, acquired informally and put to work to produce one-off pieces. The fruits of this approach have included standard lamps constructed from laminated honeycomb metals (devised by the aerospace industry for lightweight high-performance aircraft floors), as well as stainless steel chairs that redeployed a woven metal originally envisaged for use as industrial conveyor belts. It gave Arad a toehold on the production values of the modern world, without requiring him to acquire the resources needed to produce such sophisticated objects by himself. And in the nature of things, he had a tendency to treat these often fragile, sophisticated materials with a certain roughness, leading to harsh jagged edges and bruised surfaces.

The Red Tape project questioned the role of found materials from quite a different direction. It was about volume production right from the start, and was based on the aesthetics of discretion, rather than of display. With the runaway success of the Bookworm under his belt, Arad was no longer a designer who operated on the edge of industrial design. He had demonstrated that he could work in the mainstream as well.

The CD rack, eventually adopted for manufacture by Alessi, is an example of a product that conspicuously distances itself from the object fetishism of the 1980s. It is all but invisible. It does something useful with maximum economy of means. It is a storage system unlike virtually every other, that is designed to not draw attention to itself. You see neither the rack, nor the supports that keep it in position, just the CDs themselves. This is in fact the kind of object that would have been all but impossible to sell in the 1980s. It is based on a proprietary adhesive tape, manufactured by the American giant 3M, to which are applied strips of extruded plastic spacing devices. The result is a curling, flexible strip which, counter-intuitively, becomes rigid and firm only when the CD boxes are put into position. Tape it to a hard surface, slip in the CD boxes, and you have the most minimal of storage systems. When it is empty, it looks like a close relative of the Bookworm, on a miniature scale. With the CD boxes in position, it has another identity.

Arad's initial thought was to interest the adhesive manufacturer. 'Too complicated for us,' was the reply, after a protracted correspondence. However, Alessi, a company that more than any other had made its reputation with high-concept objects, was now ready to work on an object that was, almost, nothing. All it needed to complete the product was Javier Mariscal's involvement to help Arad package it in a way that could communicate the product's potential. And Mariscal's seductive doodling created a pack that brought Arad's design to life.

The Soundtrack, Alessi, 1998 (above left). A functional product, reduced to its absolute minimum, the Soundtrack is a flexible, self-adhesive strip that can be cut to length and fixed to virtually any horizontal surface. A single OD jewel case contains a 120-centimetre (47-inch) length which can store over 80 CDs between its teeth. The accompanying graphics are by Javier Mariscal. Chain Chain Chain, Alessi, 1998 (opposite) is a vertical CD storage system.

22

THREE-MINUTE EGGS

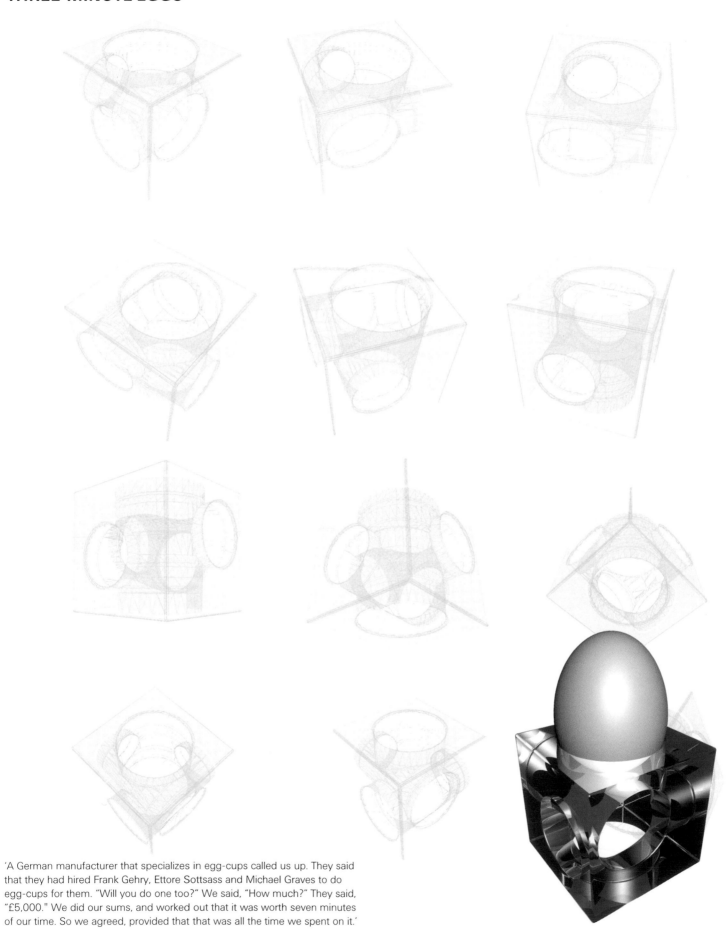

'A German manufacturer that specializes in egg-cups called us up. They said that they had hired Frank Gehry, Ettore Sottsass and Michael Graves to do egg-cups for them. "Will you do one too?" We said, "How much?" They said, "£5,000." We did our sums, and worked out that it was worth seven minutes of our time. So we agreed, provided that that was all the time we spent on it.'

Champagne glass, Leonardo, 1998 (left). The glass is designed to prevent dripping, sticky fingers. The glass is double-skinned so that any effervescence from the champagne overflows into an outer chamber. Vase, Rosenthal, 1998 (below). A stainless steel spring can be screwed up out of this porcelain vase in order to accommodate taller flowers.

Limited edition book box, 1998 (left). The box has three magnifying lenses which allow a sneak preview of the front cover.

Half a Dozen, Leonardo, Germany, 1996 (previous page). This eggcup is a cube with vaguely conical excavations on its six sides to take eggs of varying sizes. Although designed to be made in glass, production proved too difficult and the final product was made in transparent polished acrylic.

Teaset, Leonardo, 1998 (above). The baseless glass teapot rocks slightly, but however much it rocks the liquid never pours out. Palindrome, Alessi, 1998 (below left). A teapot with identical and interchangeable handle and spout. Table set, Rosenthal (below). All the pieces are made in an identical shape but are cut in different places to create a variety relating to the function of each piece.

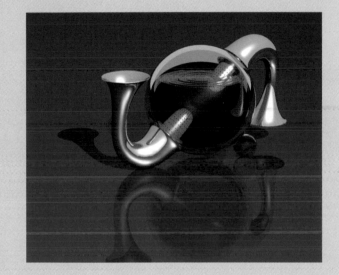

PePPer SuGAR VINAGER OIL   SALT

Martell, 1996 (above). A standard
Martell flask Cognac bottle
redesigned to provide a unique
image to promote Martell's latest
product aimed at the younger
market. The bottle contains a
floating stainless steel brand label
and is capped with a frosted glass
drinking cup incorporating a lens
in the base. Door handle, Valli &
Valli, 1998 (below). Although cast
in stainless steel, the handle is
conceived as a pressed and folded
lozenge shape. It was part of a
range of door furniture. Paint it
Ain't, Lippert Wilkins Partner,
1990 (bottom). A series of
paperweights produced by filling
aluminium paint tubes with lead.
The lead is cast into squashed,
empty tubes so that although all
the paperweights are made in
an identical way, no two are the
same.

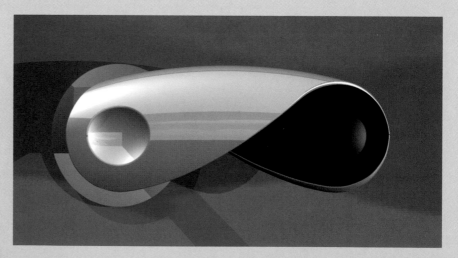

Mr Key, Heller, New York, 1997 (above). A transparent frame containing the user's local street plan and a magnetic ring that stays in one place. The map moves so that the ring records where the user's car is parked. The magnet is strong enough to hold a bunch of keys. Toilet, Allia, France, 1995 (above right). A double-skinned, egg-shaped toilet which was cantilevered for the German market and supported on two legs for the French market.

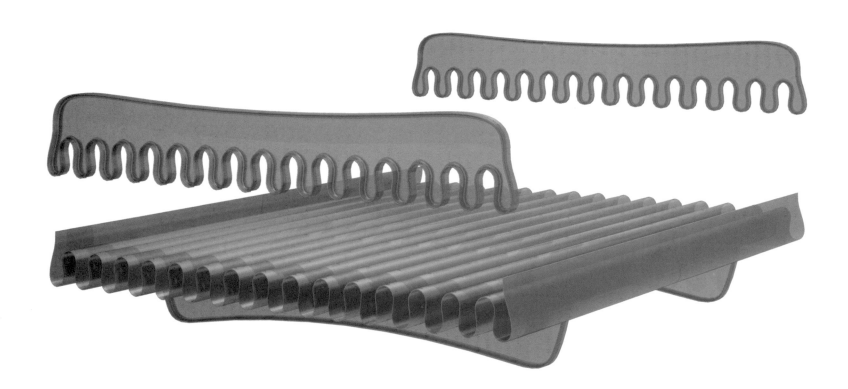

Bed, 1998 (opposite). Computer visuals showing the component parts of a bed to be produced entirely in plastic. The parts are designed to click together without the need for tools. Bookworm, Kartell, 1994 (above and below). This flexible translucent plastic strip shelving with 'book' wall brackets is different with every installation (see page 103).

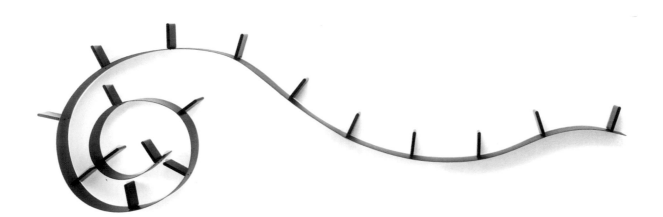

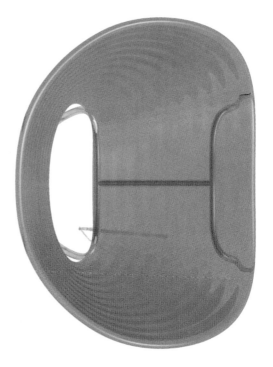

Tom Vac chair, Vitra, 1998. Just over a year after the launch of the aluminium Tom Vac and following intensive development, prototyping and adjustment by Ron Arad's team and the technical experts at Vitra, the industrialized, injection-moulded plastic Tom Vac was launched on the market. While the spirit of the original design has been retained, the shape has been refined and its comfort improved. The result is a chair that is generous in size, light-weight, stackable and affordable. Tom Vac table, Vitra. An 80cm x 80cm (31¹/₂in) table to accompany the Tom Vac chair. The top is a translucent plastic hollow box containing in its cavity part of the steel structure, allowing the same top to have either a pedestal base or four legs. The deep sloping edges of the top, with their ribs fanning out to the corners and their opposing curvature, allow tables to be joined in a variety of configurations.

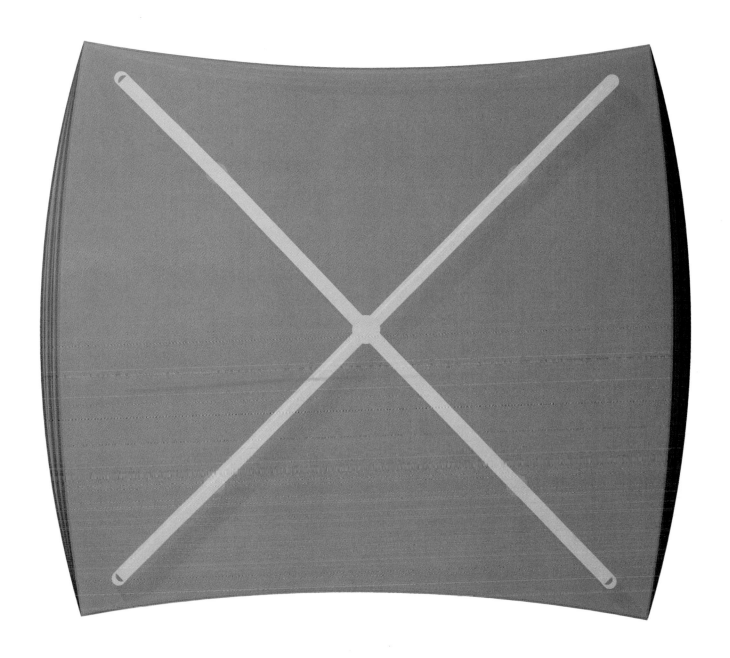

Magazine rack, 1998 (opposite). A springy, floor-standing magazine rack in lens-effect transparent 'memory' plastic. FPE stool and lounger, 1998 (below). Following on from the success of the FPE chair (see page 141), the same double-barrelled aluminium extrusion is here used for a high bar stool. Additional tooling costs have been avoided as the coloured plastic seat is exactly that used for the FPE chair.

Wine rack, 1998 (below). Modular snap-together wine storage that can 'grow' as required. H-Shelving, 1998 (above and opposite). A simple, corrugated H-shaped shelving system which allows 'H' units to be placed and stacked as desired to fit any space. No fixings are required so the configurations can be changed as needed.

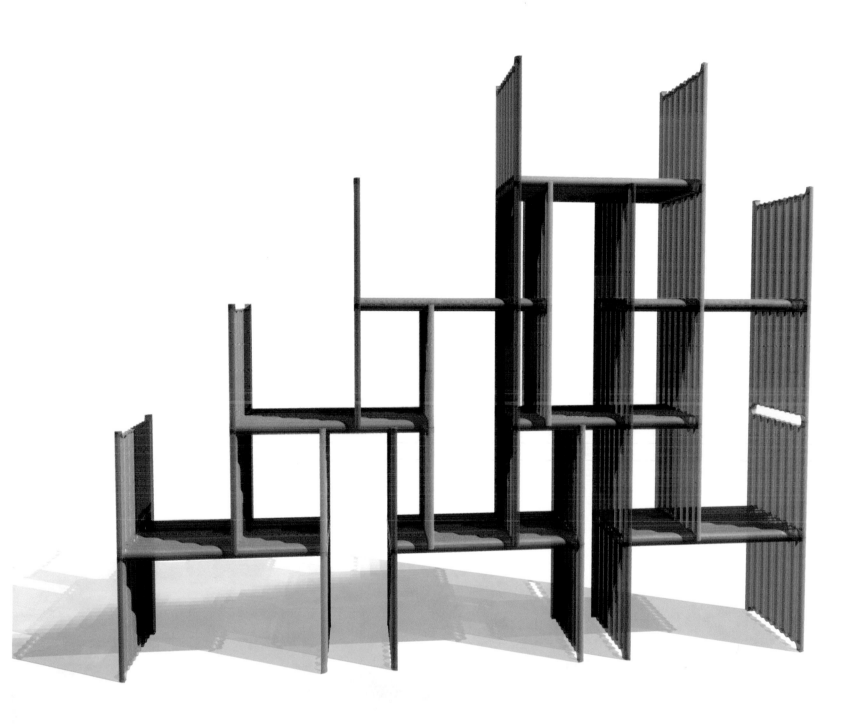

24

B.O.O.P.S

Blown out of Proportion – or B.O.O.P. – is a series of objects that have the uncanny feel that they are the physical realization of a virtual object, the condensation of a piece of liquid cyberspace. And in a way that is exactly what they are, designed in a series of computer visualizations, and reproduced in a catalogue which was printed before the pieces were actually made. The visualizations also provide the information used for a computer to carve a mould. The same technology – aluminium blow moulding technique – was used by Nicholas Grimshaw and other architects to make tightly radiussed lightweight high-tech architectural cladding, but has been transformed by Arad into a completely different entity by boosting the scale, and introducing a quality of randomness. The starting point is a piece of sheet aluminium 6mm thick, smeared with graphite. The metal is heated in an oven and put under air pressure into a template.

There is no waste as the finished pieces are assembled from every scrap. Arad limited the variables to just three mould plates, that were made reversible; one side can be more inflated than the other. 'It was all theory, we didn't know it was going to work, until we had done it. The skill you need in manufacturing this is driving a fork lift. It is a process not unlike a jelly mould used to make the body panels of a car.'

The difference is the curiously uncategorizable forms that Arad has come up with, the way he has cut and welded segments together. And most of all the laborious finishing of the pieces after the shapes have been blown, almost like the old One Off workshop days, to achieve the brilliant mirror finish, some pieces with sprayed colour on the interior faces. The collection, made for Ernest Moormans, includes a variety of dishes and plates whose primary purpose is their extraordinary tactile quality. Arad used a similar technique to create a pair of virtual fireplaces for a private house in west London.

B.O.O.P. collection, 1998. A coffee table made of two blow-formed shapes (left). Both shapes are cut to the same outline of overlapping circles. The top layer is blown very shallow and the bottom layer is deeper. When welded together they create a volume. A giant floor bowl created from a single sheet of 4mm thick blow-formed mirror-polished aluminium (below). Each compartment is blown to a different size so the bowl stands tilted on the floor. A giant, 2.5-metre (8-foot) high floor vase (opposite). Here the template was turned over to obtain a left- and right-hand side blow-formed shape.

Vases from the B.O.O.P. collection
and a coffee table (above) made
from B.O.O.P. off-cuts welded
together and polished.

A double-blown B.O.O.P. console table (opposite). One of the giant vases photographed outside the Krizia space in Milan (left).

Series of double-skinned enamel-painted coffee tables with a variety of perforation (below and following pages). A coffee table with a shallow top and a deep base (opposite).

Giant floor vases from the B.O.O.P.
collection.

THE PIPER PROJECT

Lofts are common enough in London to be taken for granted. In fact Nigel Coates's extension to the Geffrye Museum includes a loft with all the usual signifiers: maple strip floor, industrial light fittings and all, as the last of its series of twentieth-century room sets, neatly suggesting that the loft movement has already turned into a period piece. It has however transformed large areas of London. The first lofts were in Docklands, carved out of derelict warehouses by artists living without the benefit of planning permission in their workspaces. Then the movement was commercialized as developers moved in. What were initially presented as the means to an alternative lifestyle – with wide open indoor spaces offering a luxurious escape from suburban conformity – were swiftly diluted as lofts became smaller and smaller under financial pressure to make a return. The Piper House is a third generation loft, situated in a desirable part of west London, rather than an industrial wasteland. It is a building of some architectural character – named for the John Piper mural that graces it – and a number of different architects have been involved in fitting out the various apartments.

Ron Arad was asked to fit out one of the shell spaces. The loft is handsomely proportioned, but not quite tall enough to include the full second storey necessary to fulfil the client's space requirements. In response Arad has pulled off a spatial conjuring trick, fitting a twisted hull into a box. He has created a balance of public and private space by fitting what amounts to an independent structure into the bigger space, a little in the manner of the Tel Aviv Opera House foyer. The curved partitions and the boomerang kitchen worktop show Arad's signature geometry, but this is a place to live, not a sculpture.

Arad compares the upper level to a convertible car with the top down. If you stand up, your guests can see your head over the top of the balustrade, but it is private enough to sleep in, and not have people see your bed.

Penthouse flat, Piper Building,
London, 1998. View of the
hollowed-out mezzanine above
the dining area (opposite). The
transforming hull section provides
various degrees of privacy
without actually enclosing the
spaces of the mezzanine. The
mirror-polished stainless steel
dining table previously formed
part of the Fondation Cartier
installation (below left).

Ground-floor plan showing the
mezzanine structure dividing the
space into private rooms and
main living areas (below). The
kitchen and dining areas below
the mezzanine (opposite).

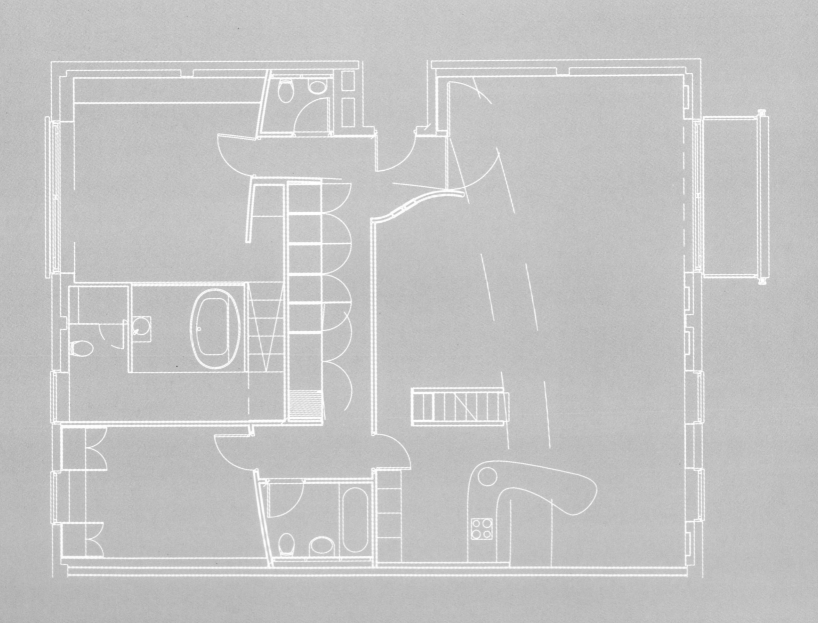

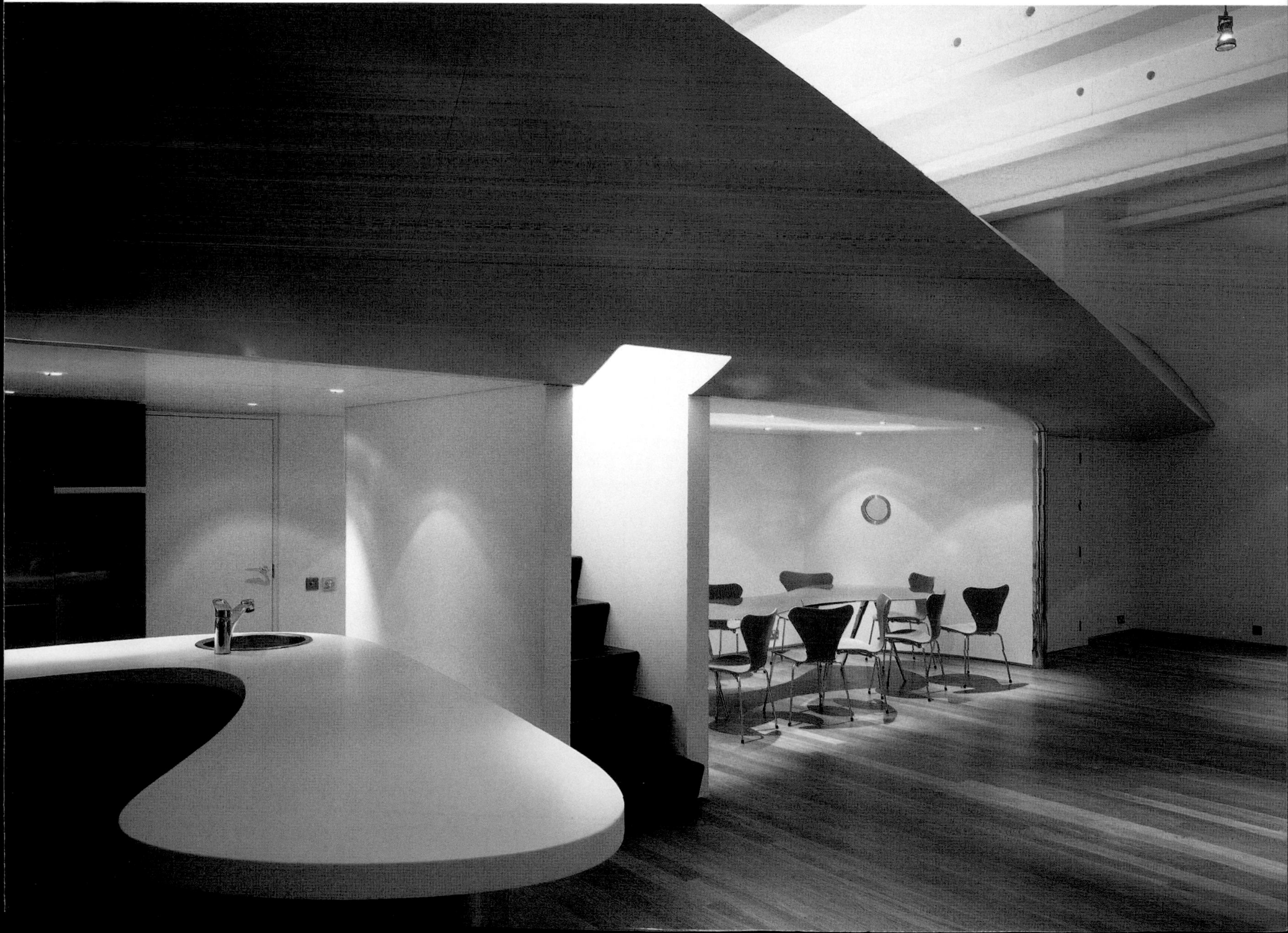

INDEX

Page numbers in italics refer to illustrations

Adidas 133
    Sports Cafés 133, *137*, *138*
    Stadium (unbuilt) 133, *135*, 135–6, *136*, *137*
Aerial Light *11*, 12, *12*
After Spring (rocking daybed) *60*
Alchymia 191
Alessi 69
    The Soundtrack (CD rack) 181, *183*
    teapot *187*
Amiga House, London 171–2, *172*, *175*, *176*
And The Rabbit Speaks (chair) 79, *82*
Arad Associates, Chalk Farm 29, *33*, *35*
Arflex 69
Arribas, Alfredo 133
Artifort 77
Aulenti, Gae 87

balustrade, conical 23, *25*
bar designs 77, *79*
beds:
    After Spring (rocking daybed) *60*
    plastic 191, *193*
Belgo Centraal, Covent Garden, London *84*
Belgo Noord restaurant, London 77, *84*, 117
    table 117, *122*, *123*
Bellini, Mario 37, 69, 87
Beware of the Dog (seating) *45*
Big Easy (Volumes series chair) *54*, 56, *56*
Bischofsburger, Bruno 49–50
Blair, Tony 171
Blown out of Proportion *see* B.O.O.P.
book box *186*
bookcases:
    One Way or Another 105, *105*
    This Mortal Coil *104*, 105
Bookworm (shelving) 103, 105–6, *106*, *193*
B.O.O.P. collection 201
    coffee tables *202*, *205*, *208*, *209*, *210–11*
    console table *207*
    vases *202*, *205*, *206*, *212*, *213*
box, book *186*
Box in Four Movements (chair) 79, *81*
Branzi, Andrea 69
Brody, Neville 91
Burckhardt, François 153

Carbo Tom (chair) *158*
Cartier tables *see* Fondation Cartier
Cassina *64*, 69
Castiglioni brothers 10, 37, 69
CD rack 181, *182*, *183*
Chain Chain Chain (CD rack) *183*
chairs and seating systems:
    And The Rabbit Speaks 79, *82*
    Beware of the Dog *45*
    Big Easy (Volumes series) *54*, 56, *56*
    Box in Four Movements 79, *81*
    Carbo Tom *158*
    Chair by its Cover *125*
    Cone chair 23
    Cross Your T's *143*
    Eight By One *67*

Empty Chair *111*
Fantastic Plastic Elastic (FPE) chair, Kartell *138*,
    141, *143*, *144*
Full House 49, *50*
Horn chair *27*
Italian Fish *64*
Let Sleeping Dogs Lie *45*
Little Heavy (Volumes series) *59*
Looming Lloyd *63*
Misfits *73*
Old Dog, New Tricks *45*
Pic Chairs *162*
Reflection on Another Chair *125*
Rolling Volume *63*
Rover chair 9, *10*, 12, 55
Schizzo chair *47*, *82*
School chair *47*
Sit! *45*
Size 10 *60*
Sof-Sofs *71*
Spanish Made *63*
Spring Collection (chairs) *74*
A Suitable Case 79, *82*
Tom Vac chairs *47*, 153, 155, *155*, *157*, *166*,
    194
Transformer 12, *15*
2Rnot *64*
Uncut *165*
Volumes series 53, *54*, 55–6, *56*, *59*
Well Tempered chair 37–8, *38*, *41*, *47*
Why Bark? Why Dog? *125*
Zigo and Zago chairs *111*
    see also stools
champagne glass (Leonardo) *186*
Citterio, Antonio 37
coffee tables (B.O.O.P.) 201, *202*, *205*, *208*
Cologne Furniture Fair 1998 155
Concrete Stereo 17, *19*
Cone chair 23
Cone tables 23, *27*
console table (B.O.O.P.) *206*
Cross Your T's (chair) *143*

Dassault, Marcel 153
daybed, rocking *60*
Documenta Kassel (1987) 49–50, *50*
door handle (Valli & Valli) *188*
Domus (magazine) 153
    Totem *85*, 153, *155*, *166*, *167*, *168*, *169*
Draenert Studio, Germany *79*
Driade 103, 109
    The Empty Chair *111*
    Zigo and Zago chairs *111*

egg-cups *185*, *186*
Ehrloff, Michael 49
Eight By One (chairs) *67*
Empty Chair, The *111*
English Heritage 172

Fantastic Plastic Elastic (FPE):
    chair *138*, 141, *143*, *144*
    lounger *197*
    stool *197*

Fehlbaum, Rolf 37, 43, 50
Fiam 109
Fly on the Wall (shelving) *81*
Fly Ply table *111*
Fondation Cartier, Paris 115
    tables 115–17, *116*, *118*, *122*
FPE *see* Fantastic Plastic Elastic
Full House (installation) 49, *50*
Future Systems 49

Gaultier, Jean-Paul 10
Gaultier for Women, London *19*, *20*
Gehry, Frank 37, 185
Graves, Michael 185
Grimshaw, Nicholas 201
Guzzini 109

H-Shelving 191, *198*
Half a Dozen (egg-cup) *186*
handrail, conical 23, *25*
hi-fi system, concrete 17, *19*
Hollein, Hans 87
Horn chairs *27*
houses:
    Amiga House 171–2, *172*, *175*, *176*
    private house/publishing studio, Germany
    179

Ikea PS range 109
Italian Fish (chair) *64*

Kartell 103, 191
    Bookworm shelving 103, 105–6, *106*, *193*
    Fantastic Plastic Elastic (FPE) chair *138*, 141,
    143, *144*
    RTW (wheel storage unit) 147, *150*
Kassel *see* Documenta Kassel
Kee Klamp scaffolding 10, 23, 191
Keenan, Berni 135
Koons, Jeff 117
Kuramata, Shiro 37

lamps *see* lights
Leonardo:
    champagne glass *186*
    egg cup *186*
    teaset *187*
Let Sleeping Dogs Lie (seating) *45*
lights:
    Aerial Light *11*, 12, *12*
    Tree Light *20*
Little Heavy (Volumes series chair) *59*
Looming Lloyd (chair) *63*
Louisiana Museum of Modern Art, Denmark 127,
    129
lounger, FPE *197*
Lovegrove, Ross 171

magazine rack *196*
Magistretti, Vico 69
Mandelson, Peter 171
Mariscal, Javier 181, *183*
Martell (Cognac bottle) *188*
Marzorati Ronchetti 79, *79*, *84*, 91, 135

Domus Totem *85*, 153, *155*, *166*, *168*
   see also Ronchetti, Stefano
Maurer, Ingo 91, *121*
Memphis 69, 191
Mendini, Alessandro 69
Mercatali, Davide 77
Mercedes Benz 141, *143*
Michelle ma Belle, Milan (shop) 93, *101*
Milan:
   Domus Totem *85*, 153, *155*, *166*, *168*
   Furniture Fairs 77, 153, 191
   Triennale (1995): '38 Tables' *118*, *121*
Miller, Herman 37
Mini-Bookworm (shelving) 105, *105*
Misfits (seating system) *73*
Moormans, Ernest 201
Moroso 69, 103
   Misfits (seating) *73*
   Sof-Sofs (seating) *71*
   Spring Collection (chairs) *74*
Morrison, Jasper 49
Mortal Coil, the *see* This Mortal Coil
Mourmans Gallery *162*

Narrow Papardelle (chair) *67*
Nouvel, Jean 133
   Fondation Cartier, Paris 115

Old Dog, New Tricks (seating) *45*
One Off 9, 10, 53
   Neal Street 10, 17, 23, *25*, *31*
   Shelton Street *32*
One Way or Another (bookcase) 105, *105*

Paint it Ain't (paperweights) *188*
Palindrome (Alessi) *187*
Papardelle *see* Narrow Papardelle
Pawson, John 171
Pesce, Gaetano *64*, 191
Pic Chairs *162*
Piper project 215, *217*, *218*
Pompidou Centre exhibition (1987) 49
   Sticks and Stones (installation) 50, *51*
Prouvé, Jean 12
   armchair 12
   Compass table *121*
Puch stool 12, *20*

Radice, Barbara 191
Reflection on Another Chair (chairs) *125*
Rolling Volume (rocking armchair) *63*
Ronchetti, Stefano 77, 89
   see also Marzorati Ronchetti
Rosenthal:
   table set *187*
   vase *186*
Rover chair 9, *10*, 12, 55
RTW (wheel storage unit) 147, *150*

Salway, Oliver 135
Schizzo chairs *47*, *82*
Schnabel and Kieffer 50
School chair *47*
Science Museum, London 127, *131*

seating *see* chairs and seating systems; sofa;
stools
Seifert, John 172
Serpentine Gallery, London: 'Vessels' exhibition
25
Shadow of Time 23, *25*
shelving:
   The Bookworm 103, 105–6, *106*, *193*
   Fly on the Wall *81*
   H-Shelving *198*
   Mini-Bookworm 105, *105*
Sipek, Borek 77
Sit! (seating) *45*
Size 10 (armchair) *60*
Smith, Chris 171
Sof-Sofs (seating) *71*
sofa, St.St. *79*
Sottsass, Ettore 37, 69, 185, 191
   Valentine typewriter 9
Soundtrack (CD rack) 181, *183*
Spanish Made (chair) *63*
Spring Collection (chairs) *74*
staircases:
   Neal Street shop 23, *25*, *31*
   Tel Aviv Opera House *79*, 95
Starck, Philippe 49, 191
stereo, concrete 17, *19*
Sticks and Stones (installation) 50, *51*
stools:
   FPE *197*
   Puch 12, *20*
storage:
   magazine rack *198*
   Soundtrack (CD rack) 181, *183*
   wheeled unit 147, *150*
   wine rack *198*
   see also shelving
St.St. sofa *79*
Suitable Case, A (case/chair) 79, *82*
Superform Aluminium 153

T44 (tea trolley) *111*
table set (Rosenthal) *187*
tables:
   Cartier 115–17, *116*, *118*, *122*
   coffee tables (B.O.O.P. collection) 201, *202*,
   205, *208*
   Cone 23, *27*
   console table (B.O.O.P. collection) *206*
   Fly Ply table *111*
   '38 Tables' installation (Milan Triennale) *118*,
   121
   Tom Vac table *194*
Taylor, Gerry 49
tea trolley, T44 *111*
teapot (Palindrome, Alessi) *187*
teaset (Leonardo) *187*
Tel Aviv Opera House 79, 87, 89, 91, 93
   amphitheatre staircase *79*, 95
   bookshop *96*, 97
   box office *93*
   bronze wall *79*, *96*
   foyer 87, *89*
   'island' *89*, *91*, *98*

This Mortal Coil (bookcase) *104*, 105
Thomas, Neil 29
toilet *188*
Tom Vac chairs *47*, 153, 155, *155*, *157*, *166*, *194*
   Carbo Tom *158*
   Uncut *165*
Tom Vac table *194*
Toulon, France: Adidas Sport Café *138*
Transformer (seating) 12, *15*
Tree Light *20*
trolley, T44 *111*
2Rnot (chairs) *64*

Uncut (chair) *165*

vases:
   B.O.O.P. *202*, *205*, *206*, *211*
   Rosenthal *186*
Victor, Eric 12
Vitra 37, 38, *41*, *45*, 155
   Schizzo chair *47*, *82*
   Tom Vac chairs *47*, 153, 155, *155*, *157*, *158*,
   165, *166*, *194*
   Tom Vac table *194*
Vitra Design Museum, Weil am Rhein *50*
Volumes series chairs 53, *54*, 55–6, *56*, *59*
Vuitton, Louis 50

Waterlily (ICI material) *73*
Weil, Daniel 49
Well Tempered chair 37–8, *38*, *41*, *47*
Werwerka, Stefan 49
wheel storage units 147, *150*
Why Bark? Why Dog? (chairs) *125*
Wilson, Richard: bath of sump oil and steel 117,
121
wine rack *198*

Zeus 77, 191
Zigo and Zago chairs *111*

BIOGRAPHY

1951	Born in Tel Aviv
1971–73	Studied at the Jerusalem Academy of Art
1973	Moved to London
1974–79	Studied at the Architectural Association, School of Architecture
1981	With Caroline Thorman established One Off Ltd, a design studio, workshops and showroom in Covent Garden
1989	With Caroline Thorman founded Ron Arad Associates, an architecture and design practice in Chalk Farm
1993	One Off incorporated into Ron Arad Associates
1994	Ron Arad Studio established in Como, Italy, to continue and expand on the production studio pieces as previously produced in the London workshops
1994–97	Professor of Product Design at the Hochschule in Vienna
1997	Professor of Furniture Design at the Royal College of Art, London
1998–	Professor of Industrial Design and Furniture Design at the Royal College of Art, London.

CHRONOLOGY OF MAJOR WORKS

Furniture and Products

1981	Rover chair
	Aerial Light
	The Transformer
1983	Concrete Stereo
1985	Cone tables and Horn chairs
1986	The Shadow of Time
1986	The Well Tempered chair, Vitra Editions
	The School chair, Vitra Editions
1988	The Big Easy, Rolling Volume, Italian Fish and Size 10 chairs (Volumes series)
1989	Schizzo chair, Vitra Editions
	Little Heavy chair
	Looming Lloyd chair
	Chair by its Cover, Why Bark?, Why Dog? and Reflection on Another Chair series
1990	Beware of the Dog, Old Dog New Tricks, Let Sleeping Dogs, Sit! (Vitra workshop pieces)
	Spanish Made chair (Volumes series)
	The Spring Collection (ten chairs), Moroso
1991	Eight By One chair
1992	After Spring daybed, 2Rnot chair and London Papardelle
1993	Misfits seating system, Moroso
	This Mortal Coil, One Way or Another and Bookworm
	Zigo and Zago chairs, Driade
1994	Fly on the Wall shelving system
	Box in Four Movements chair
	And The Rabbit Speaks chair
	A Suitable Case case/chair
	The Bookworm shelving, Kartell
	The Empty Chair, T44 trolley and Fly Ply table, Driade
1995	Sof-Sofs seating system, Moroso
	Cler shelving/display system, Fiam
1996	Cross Your T's chair
	RTW storage wheels
1997	Fantastic Plastic Elastic chair (FPE), Kartell
	Tom Vac chair, Carbo Tom chair, Pic Chairs and Uncut chair
1998	The Soundtrack CD storage, Alessi
	Tom Vac chair, Vitra (in injection-moulded plastic) and Tom Vac table
	B.O.O.P. (Blown out of Proportion) collection (coffee tables, floor bowls and vases)

Architecture and Installations

1983, 1986	One Off showrooms, Neal Street and Shelton Street, Covent Garden
1986	Bazaar, Gaultier for Women boutique, London
1990	Philips Electronic Exhibition, Berlin
1993	Michelle ma Belle fashion shop, Via della Spiga, Milan
1991	Ron Arad Associates Studios, Chalk Farm, London (with Alison Brooks)
1994	Belgo bar and restaurant extension, Chalk Farm, London (with Alison Brooks)
1989–94	Foyer architecture for the new Tel Aviv Opera House, Israel (with Alison Brooks)
1995	Office 'Y' Building, Seoul, Korea (in conjunction with David Chipperfield Architects)
	Belgo Centraal restaurant, Covent Garden (with Alison Brooks and Monique van den Hurk)
	Galerie Achenbach, Düsseldorf (art gallery)
1995–96	Adidas Stadium, Paris (winning scheme in invited competition – unbuilt)
1996	Adidas/Kronenbourg Sports Cafés, France
	Exhibition design for British room in the 'Design and Identity' exhibition,
	Louisiana Museum of Modern Art, Denmark
	Proposal for stand for Mercedes Benz AG, Birmingham Motor Show
1997	Private residence, London (with Barnaby Gunning)
	Conversion of top floors of a Victorian house, Haverstock Hill, London
	Scheme for office reception area, 14–15 Conduit Street, London
	Spatial elements and furniture for private residence, Israel
	Domus Totem, Milan
	Shortlisted in competition for 'Making the Modern World' gallery, Science Museum, London (with Barnaby Gunning)
1998	Penthouse flat, Piper Building, London (with Geoff Crowther)
1999	Exhibition design for 'Winning. The Design of Sports', Glasgow 1999 UK City of Architecture and Design (with Barnaby Gunning and Geoff Crowther)
	Meteor Alsatian Restaurant, London (with Barnaby Gunning)
	Various projects, Canary Wharf, London (with Barnaby Gunning)

Major Exhibitions

1986	'Intellectual Interiors', Tokyo (with Philippe Starck, Rei Kawakubo, Shiro Kuramata)
1987	Documenta 8, Kassel
	'Nouvelles Tendances', Pompidou Centre, Paris
1990	'Ron Arad Recent Works', Tel Aviv Museum of Art
1990–95	'Sticks and Stones', Vitra Design Museum touring exhibition
1991	'A Break with Tradition', Röhsska Museet, Gothenburg
1993	'One Off and Short Runs', Centre for Contemporary Arts (Warsaw, Krakow, Prague)
	'Design in the Twentieth Century', Grand Palais
	'Breeding in Captivity', Edward Totah Gallery
1994	'L'Esprit du Nomade', Fondation Cartier, Paris
1995	'Ron Arad and Ingo Maurer', Triennale, Milan
	'The Work of Ron Arad', Museum of Applied Arts, Helsinki
	'Ron Arad', Gazi, Athens
1996	Glasgow Festival of Architecture and Design
1996/1997	'Ron Arad and Ingo Maurer', Spazio Krizia, Milan